The Art of LEGO® Construction

New York City
Brick by Brick

The Art of LEGO® Construction

New York City Brick by Brick

Jonathan Lopes

Abrams Image, New York

Editor: Garrett McGrath
Designer: Eli Mock
Production Manager: Rebecca Westall

Library of Congress Control Number: 2018936269

ISBN: 978-1-4197-3468-7
eISBN: 978-1-68335-520-5

Printed and bound in China
10 9 8 7 6 5 4 3 2 1

Abrams Image books are available at special discounts when purchased
in quantity for premiums and promotions as well as fundraising or educational
use. Special editions can also be created to specification. For details, contact
specialsales@abramsbooks.com or the address below.

ABRAMS The Art of Books
195 Broadway, New York, NY 10007
abramsbooks.com

For Greyson

Introduction

For as long as I can remember, I've been pursuing a creative and artistic life. As a child, I was enrolled in after-school art classes that covered various artistic mediums, such as painting, drawing, printmaking, and sculpture. I worked extensively with pastels, which allow for the blending of colors. They taught me about different color combinations and how colors can work together to develop subtle contrast. I loved art, but my true passion was my toy of choice: LEGO bricks. I had a large bag of LEGO pieces that were augmented a couple of times per year with LEGO kits I received as gifts. I would typically build the LEGO kits once or twice and then add the parts to my existing mix. From there I would let my imagination take over and build my own creations.

That is how things stayed until I was about eleven years old, when I discovered music. From my teens to my mid-twenties, I threw myself into it as my creative outlet and art form. This took me from Boston to Los Angeles and finally, in 1990, to New York City. After a number of years pursuing a career as a musician, I decided to develop a more stable full-time career and found my way into the book-publishing industry. It was a pivotal change for me. I was now immersed in an extremely creative field and one that offered a wide variety of avenues to explore, including graphic design, writing, paper engineering, and format development.

Music was now playing a diminished role in my life, and though the publishing career was quite rewarding, I still felt the need to create on my own. This was about the time that the LEGO company obtained its first license to manufacture building kits based on the *Star Wars* franchise. My interest was piqued, so I went out to a toy store and bought my first LEGO kit as an adult. I was quickly reacquainted with the shapes, colors, and pieces that I had known as a child and enjoyed working with them again. I purchased a number of additional kits and, more importantly, a few general mixed buckets of LEGO bricks. From there, over the course of a number of years, I regularly designed and built my own LEGO creations and shared photos of them online in LEGO fan forums. Soon I was being contacted by others to design and build things for them. Shortly thereafter I started participating in art exhibitions in New York City. This all set the foundation for my art today. The years of building as a hobbyist, unbeknownst to me at the time, helped me develop the building style and techniques that now define my work.

This book presents a collection of my New York City–inspired art. It also highlights particular building techniques I used to achieve the unique visual details that we associate with the icons of New York's cityscape. I have found that the inclusion of small details, such as air conditioner units, trees, and garbage cans, can truly bring a piece to life. But the added details should not be excessive: There is a balance that needs to be maintained between the details, the colors, and the textures. Attaining that special balance is something I strive for with each piece.

I have a very organic approach to creating with LEGO bricks. My process doesn't involve CAD programs. I prefer instead to sketch out my ideas on LEGO graph paper, which is available online. When replicating an existing structure, I research it online, and if I don't have the opportunity to physically visit it, I'll walk the perimeter using Google Street View. I use Google Earth to assess the footprint and the roof elements.

My work is meant to capture the essence of each subject, not to be a replica or a scale model. My intent is to work within the parameters of each prototype, rendering many details as accurately as I can, but I also add my own nuances, details, and interpretations to each piece. Doing so enables me to have a uniform body of work and also to leave my artistic stamp on each project.

New York City has been home to the then–tallest structure in the world numerous times over the years. It is also well-known for its spectacular bridges. Each building and each bridge stamps its own signature on this remarkable city. Though I intentionally steer away from some of the most famous buildings and structures, such as the Statue of Liberty, I have included many familiar landmarks in this book. I also like to pay attention to significant buildings that fly a bit under the radar. Each work in these pages presented its own building and design challenges and provided me with a renewed appreciation of the extraordinary architecture of New York City.

A Note About LEGO Bricks

One of the unique characteristics of LEGO bricks is that while there are many shapes and colors to choose from, not all shapes are manufactured in all LEGO colors. There may be five hundred different shapes available in one color and only fifty different shapes available in another. This is one of the challenges of working with LEGO bricks as a medium. The shape you need just might not exist in the color you need. And there are no custom-colored pieces.

I take all this into consideration as I develop and build my creations. I utilize online resources to assess what shapes are sold in each color, and work within the available palette. One of my most enjoyable experiences, in addition to seeing the completed sculpture once it is finished, is recalling the challenges I faced, and the problems I solved, while building it.

Additionally, while I use all shapes of LEGO pieces, I find some pieces to be overly specialized. I'll often try to avoid using these specialized pieces and will attempt to employ the more standard pieces to elicit the effect that the specialty pieces might have provided. In the instruction panels in this book, I share how I employ the pieces to achieve certain aesthetic results in my work.

I purchase my LEGO pieces at LEGO brand stores and also through the BrickLink website. I almost exclusively buy parts. If I buy a LEGO kit, it is because I know it includes pieces that I do not want to wait to have shipped to me by BrickLink.

In 2004, the LEGO company changed its formulas for some of the colors of the pieces and discontinued the older versions of those colors. Grays, browns, and black were affected at that time. I embraced this change and still utilize the older versions of the colors, though they are becoming increasingly rare. The older colors are much warmer in hue than the new versions.

I don't consider myself a LEGO purist. I glue my work together and also utilize steel reinforcement as needed in larger pieces. My creations are intended to be exhibited in public and need to withstand the rigors of shipping and travel. I have also embraced custom graphics and printing on LEGO bricks for some of my projects. The graphics, signage, and colors add further life and vitality to my work. In addition, some of the leaves I use on my trees are manufactured by altBricks in Portland, Oregon. While the LEGO company does make a piece in this shape, I prefer the palette that altBricks provides.

Over the years, my style has evolved to where it is today. My earlier work was based on my not wanting my audience to realize at first sight, that my projects were made with LEGO bricks. My creations were very smooth and refined, with very little LEGO stud exposure, and utilized many specialized pieces. My approach changed as I participated in more and more exhibitions. I found myself having to explain that my models indeed comprised LEGO pieces, with no custom shapes. With the progress of 3-D printing technology, I found that I was often asked if I employed 3-D printing in my art. I've since altered my creative approach, not only to include areas of LEGO stud exposure but also to reduce the number of specialty pieces used. I now want my renderings to present as, and to be understood to be, LEGO. Moreover, a technique I developed in 2010 of exposing the underside of LEGO pieces as added detail now features prominently in my work.

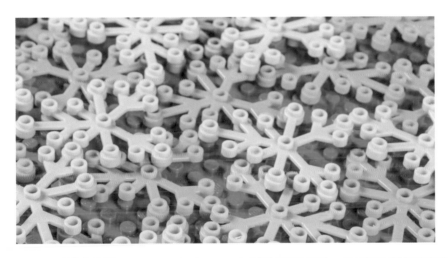

A Historic Skyline

Although I was raised in suburban Massachusetts, I've been drawn to urban environments for as long as I can remember. By the time I was fifteen, I was taking the train into Boston and Cambridge to buy records and soak in the atmosphere. In 1990, I moved to New York City and quickly immersed myself in life here. It was a natural fit for me, and I truly became myself in New York. The energy of the city resonates with me and motivates me. The diverse architecture and infrastructure is inspiring. You can walk down a single block and pass buildings and other structures that span a century. The varied details and styles of architecture complement, and sometimes conflict with, one another. This chapter focuses on some of the tallest, longest, most historic, and best-known structures in the city.

City
Hall

Completed:
May 2018

Approximate
Number of
LEGO Pieces:
18,200

Dimensions:
51"L × 28"W × 18"H
(129cm × 71cm × 46cm)

New York's City Hall, designed by architects Joseph François Mangin and John McComb Jr., was constructed in the early 1800s. It has had numerous renovations and updates since then. The building's architectural style is quite similar to that of city hall buildings in other American cities, most notably Baltimore, Maryland.

City Hall sits at the northern end of City Hall Park and above the closed but perfectly preserved 1904 City Hall subway station. It's a huge building with a large footprint and large arched windows. One of my goals was to keep this version close in scale to my other buildings, so when they are exhibited together there is consistency among them. Thus, when designing my LEGO version of this building, I had to take a bit of artistic license and forgo some of the details in the facade, though it was important to me to maintain the facade columns and ribbing on the first level. I used jumper plates with a 1 × 6 stud tile affixed to them to elicit this ribbing effect.

I also elected to design the windows three studs wide. This presented some limitations with the arches. The LEGO company makes an arch brick, but not in a three-stud-wide size. I had to design the arches myself out of plates and tiles. Additionally, because of the size of the footprint of this piece, I designed it in three modular sections that need to be assembled at exhibitions. Building in sections makes transportation easier and also allows one person to manage the setup. The larger the overall building, the more hands are needed for moving and setup.

The back entrance. Security is heavy in this area. This is where the mayor typically enters and exits the building.

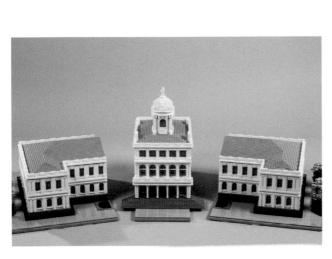

Clockwise from top right: The tower. Building all these details into a small rounded section was a challenge. Note the minifigure statue on top of the section.

The Left section. Note all the ornamental details and textures.

Because this replica is so large, I designed it and built in sections for easy transport.

Brooklyn
Bridge

At more than sixteen feet long, the
Brooklyn Bridge is the longest piece
I've created to date. Notice the
slight curve and incline in the road
deck spans.

Completed:
May 2018

Approximate
Number of
LEGO Pieces:
26,000

Dimensions:
199"L × 15"W × 26"H
(505cm × 38cm × 66cm)

The Brooklyn Bridge, which connects the boroughs of Manhattan and Brooklyn, was completed in 1883 after fourteen years of construction. The bridge was designed by John Augustus Roebling, who didn't live to see its completion. Roebling's son Washington Augustus was a civil engineer and oversaw the remainder of the construction. The original transportation methods used to cross the bridge were streetcars, elevated trains, horse and buggy, and bicycles; the bridge could also be traversed on foot. Now there are six lanes dedicated to automobiles in addition to the bicycle and pedestrian pathway in the center.

Like much of my work, this is intended to be not an exact-scale replica of the Brooklyn Bridge but, rather, a recognizable nod to the original, with my own stylings and nuances included. I based the size of my rendering on the towers. I designed and built the towers first and let them dictate the overall size of the final piece. The towers are built entirely out of LEGO plates, as opposed to LEGO bricks. The plates are one-third the height of the bricks, and using them instead of bricks created a texture that I feel closely resembles that of the bridge's actual limestone blocks. Employing plates also tripled the number of parts needed for the towers. The extra work and expense that this choice created were worth it to me when I look at the finished result.

The deck spans involved a lot of repetition building. Once I had determined the color scheme for them, I set about building the center support, then the road decks, and finally the steel cage–like infrastructure over the road decks. The center span of this piece has a steel pipe embedded in it, secured in place with epoxy. This adds stability and prevents the natural sagging that occurs when building long spans with LEGO bricks.

I truncated the footings on each end of the bridge to a reasonable size. The overall length of my model is more than sixteen feet, and I needed to stop somewhere. I did, however, include unique elements in each of the footings to represent each side of the bridge. The Manhattan side includes some very weathered building facades in its base, while the Brooklyn side has some grassy areas and also some trees abutting it.

A nice angle shot
of both towers
and decks.

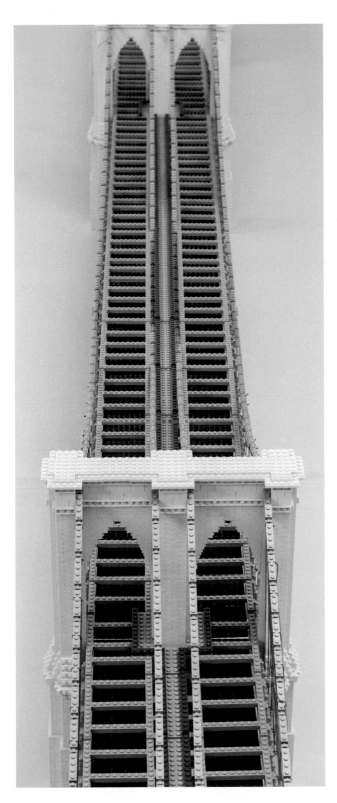

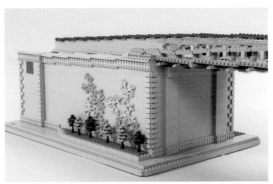

Left: Helicopter view looking down on the road decks and the grid work that encompasses them.

Top, right: The Brooklyn-side ballast anchor.

Bottom, right: The Manhattan-side ballast anchor.

Flatiron Building

Completed:	Approximate	Dimensions:
April 2018	Number of	36"L × 16"W × 46"H
	LEGO Pieces:	(91cm × 40cm × 117cm)
	71,000	

Designed by Daniel Burnham and Frederick P. Dinkelberg, the Flatiron Building was one of the tallest buildings in New York City upon its completion in 1902. Situated just south of Madison Square Park, it splits Broadway and 5th Avenue at 23rd Street as both roadways head downtown.

This building has intrigued me for years. The textures and designs on its sides are elaborate and vary extensively all the way up each facade. My design process for this rendering was similar to that for my Woolworth Building (page 70): I sketched a line of windows on paper to ensure I had the correct number of them and also an accurate amount of space between them. From there, I built a footprint mock-up to determine the size of the base. I double- and triple-checked the sizing for accuracy and then built the base and the street-level footprint. Once that was completed, I focused on one floor at a time and designed and built my way up.

To achieve the complex level of texturing of each facade, I utilized hundreds of bricks with side studs as well as Technic bricks with holes in them. I use the Technic bricks with holes in them to embed the studs of the plates in order to expose the undersides of the plates, which gives a very satisfactory texture in this scale of building. While I typically add black LEGO bricks behind the windows of my work, for my Flatiron Building I chose to use yellow bricks behind some of the windows to signify the offices of friends who work there.

Because the window spaces were based on an odd number of studs toward the top of the building, I built the arches from scratch out of LEGO pieces, as opposed to using a special LEGO arch brick; the arch brick isn't available in odd widths. The detailing of these arch panels is quite elaborate as well.

The east side
of the building
also showing
where Broadway
was repurposed
as a pedestrian
sitting area.

Left: West side of the building. Note all the textures in the facade.

Right: East side of the building with the artist in the shot to help provide the scale of the work.

Above: A nice view of the upper floors showing all the textures in the facade.

Below: Street level shot showing the east side of the building.

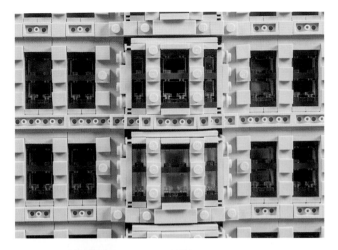

Clockwise from top left: The bay window office of a friend—note the yellow bricks used behind the window to give the impression she is in the office.

Circular window above the entrance to the building.

A section showing the many windows of this building.

Bay window detailing.

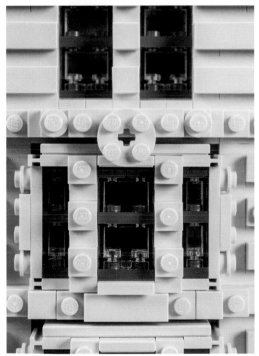

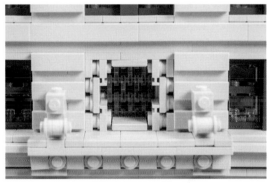

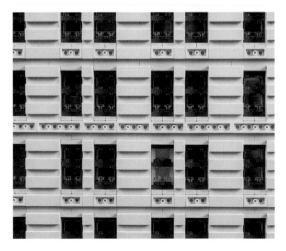

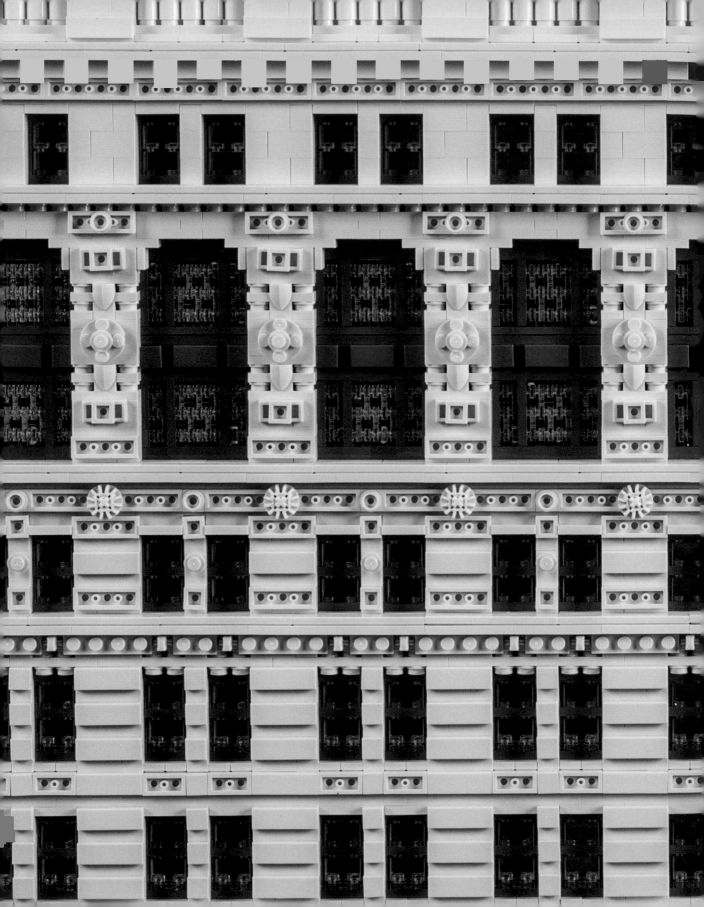

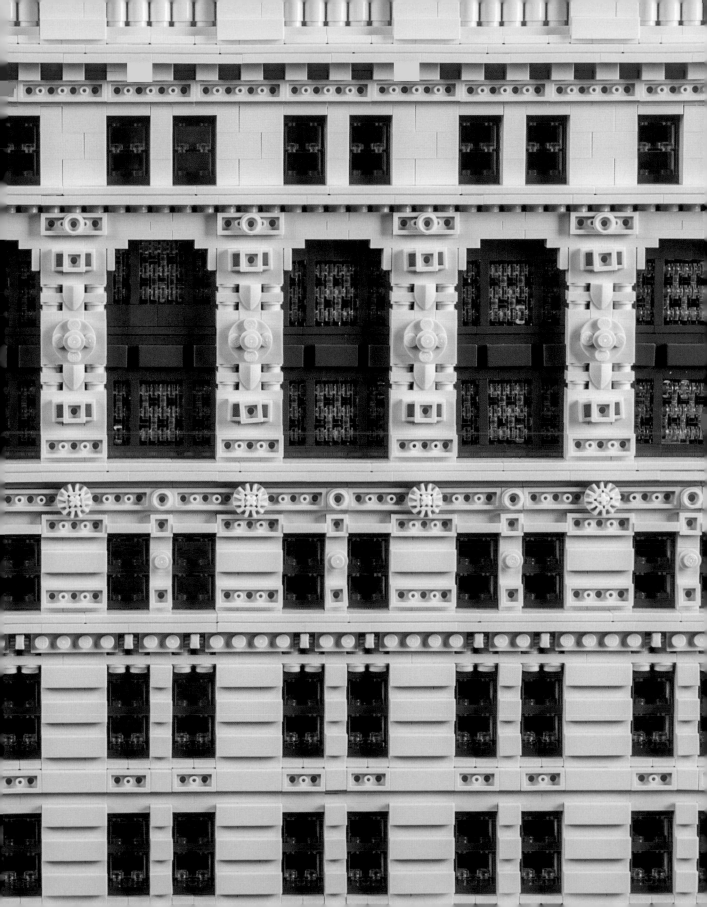

Upper facade detail

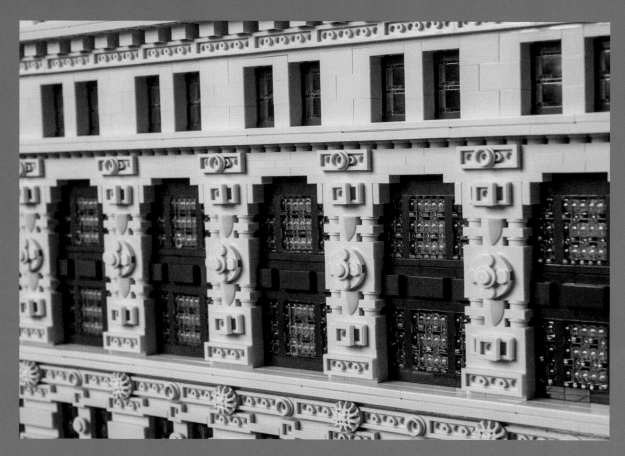

The detailing all over the facades of this building is extensive—a great creative challenge. The upper sections between the arches are an area of focus. My interpretation, using many bricks with side studs along with Technic bricks, is diagrammed in the following panels.

Closeup of the upper-floor arched windows. These are seven studs wide, so I had to replicate the arch shape using tiles and plates.

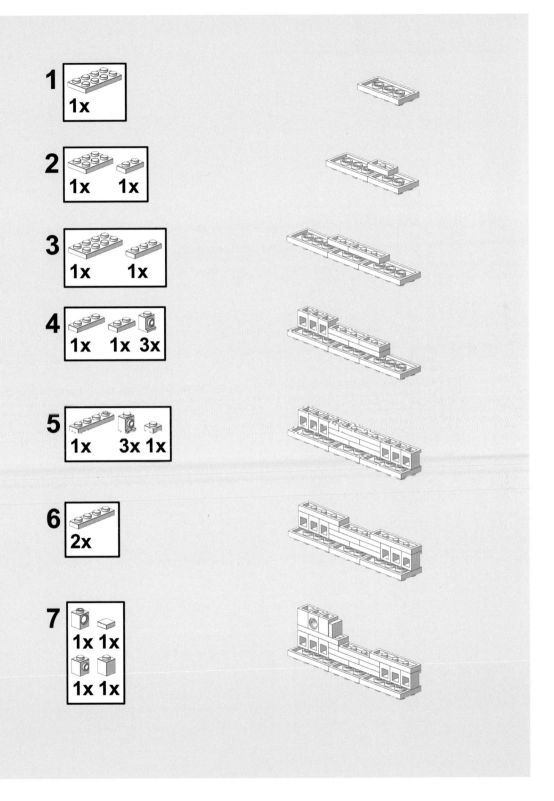

1 1x

2 1x 1x

3 1x 1x

4 1x 1x 3x

5 1x 3x 1x

6 2x

7 1x 1x
1x 1x

8 1x 1x 1x 1x

9 2x 2x

10 2x 2x

11

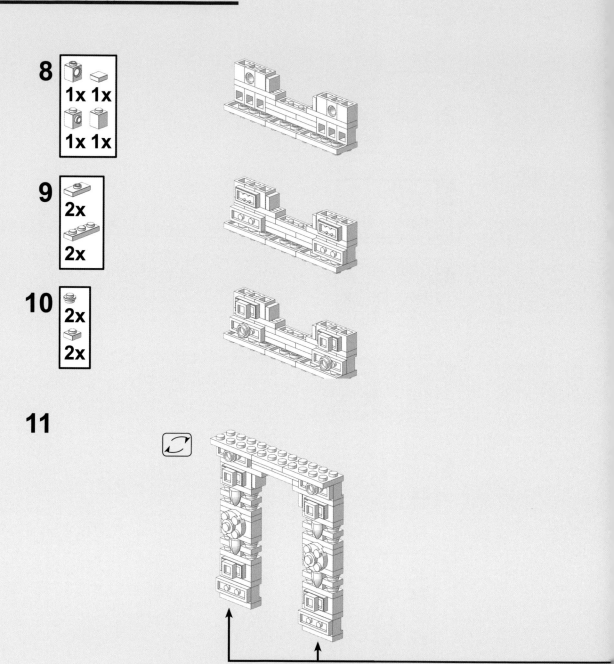

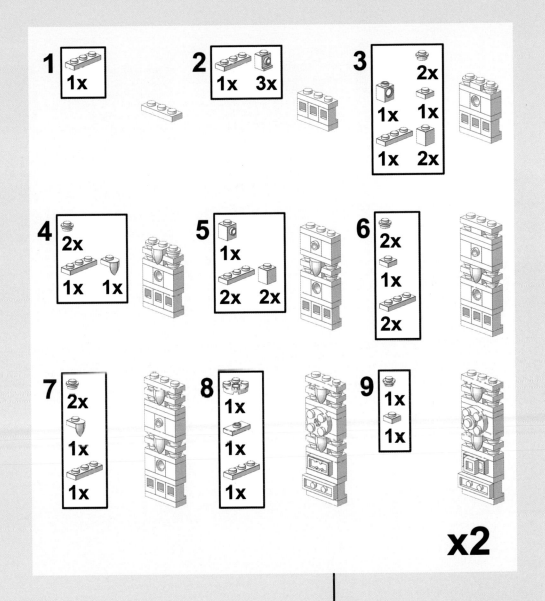

x2

Subway Entrance

Street details establish context and add life to a building, so I included subway entrances on the sidewalks of my Flatiron Building. Although they are reasonably simple builds, I made sure to add the glass lamp atop a newel post that denotes an entrance or exit.

Subway entrance. Not evident in the photos are the stairs leading down to the subway station.

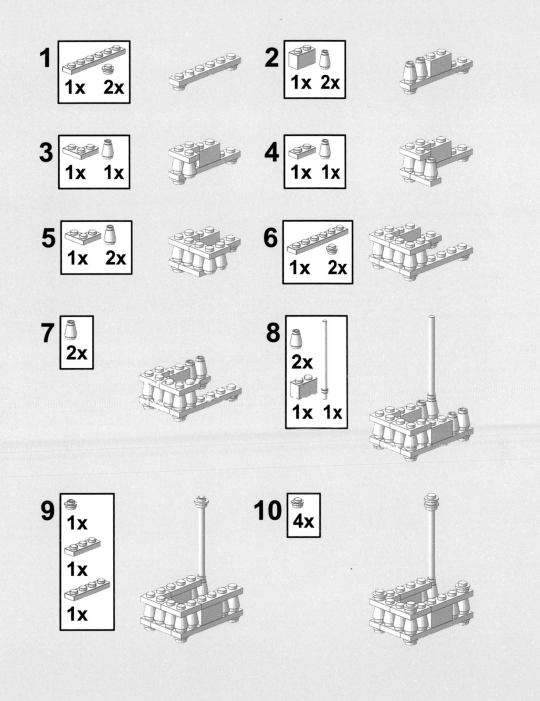

Grand Central
Terminal

Completed:
June 2017

Approximate
Number of
LEGO Pieces:
62,500

Dimensions:
**54"L × 46"W × 22"H
(137cm × 117cm × 56cm)**

I worked near Grand Central Terminal for a number of years, and it was on my "to be constructed" list for a long time. The Grand Central Terminal that we know today was designed by Reed & Stem and opened on February 2, 1913. The terminal is an amazing building. It incorporates limestone blocks typical of the era in which it was constructed but blends them with exposed girders and steelwork, presenting a truly rewarding vision of texture and coloring. I was thrilled to have the opportunity to model this building. The project was made a little easier to build because the rare LEGO color sand green had recently been made available in bulk at certain LEGO brand stores. There were only a few shapes available in this color, but all were very useful to me in this build. I utilized more than five thousand 1 × 2 plates in this sand-green color for the roof alone.

While researching this building, I learned that many of the ornamental features, though positioned in the same areas on different sides of the building, actually differ from one another. Replicating these was a bit of a visual challenge. Because they are all unique, there was a risk they would affect the visual balance of the overall piece.

A fellow artist suggested that, in order to replicate the north side of this building accurately, I research photographs of the construction of the Pan Am Building (today the MetLife Building), which is directly north of Grand Central. Images of the Pan Am Building under construction included the north side of the terminal. I don't think I'd have been able to find photos of it otherwise.

I didn't realize the back side of Grand Central Terminal was so detailed until I researched photos of the construction of the adjoining building.

Clockwise from top: The famous clock. There are lots of pieces employed here, and they're positioned at slight and unique angles. Can you see the three minifigures used in this section?

To create contrast with the smoothness of the sidewalk, I kept the studs exposed in the awnings above the street-level shops.

Inner roof area with skylights and HVAC units.

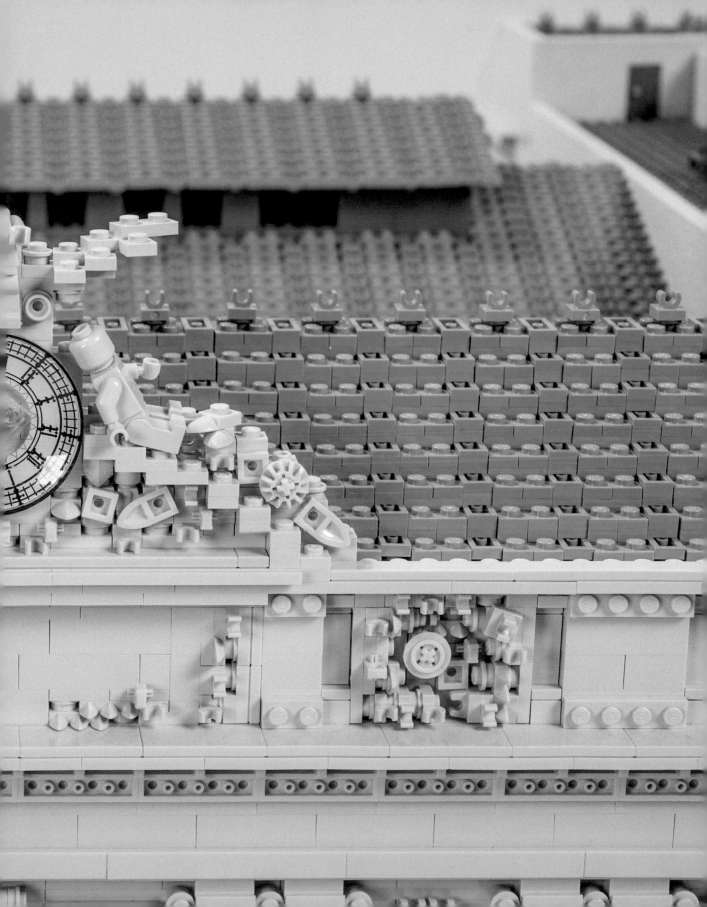

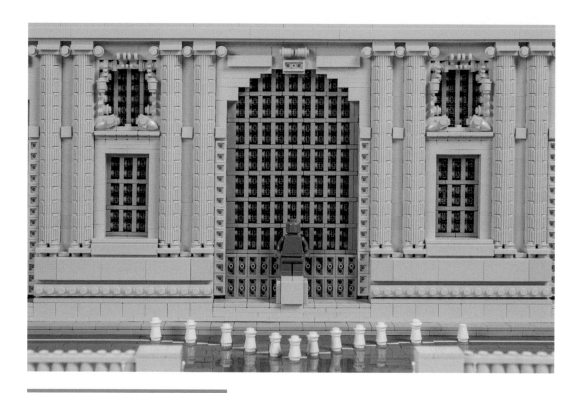

Above: Minifigure statue in front of the huge arched windows. Note that the windows are built sideways.

Opposite, above: The roof above the main concourse. When you are inside waiting for your train, you are probably standing underneath this roof!

Opposite, below: One of the many decorative ornaments that adorn the facade of Grand Central Terminal. I used the hinge plates to give the effect of the angled details.

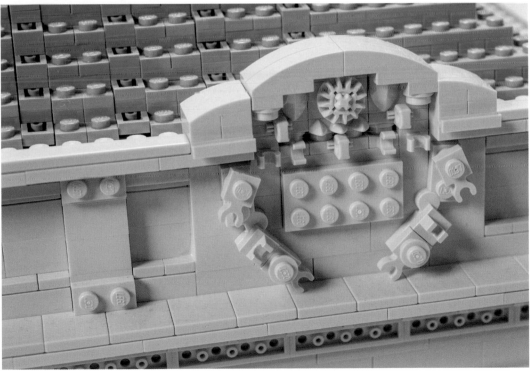

Girder

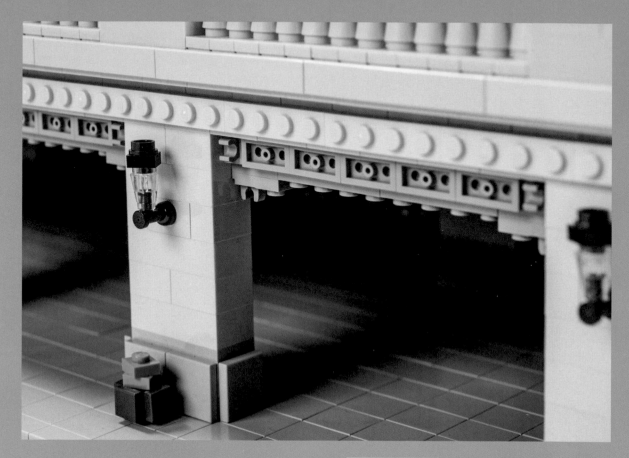

This girder is one of my favorite details on this piece. Just a few different-shape LEGO pieces are used, but the result is impressive.

Side shot, showing the girders that reinforce the structure and the street above. Note the exposed undersides of the LEGO pieces that give added detail.

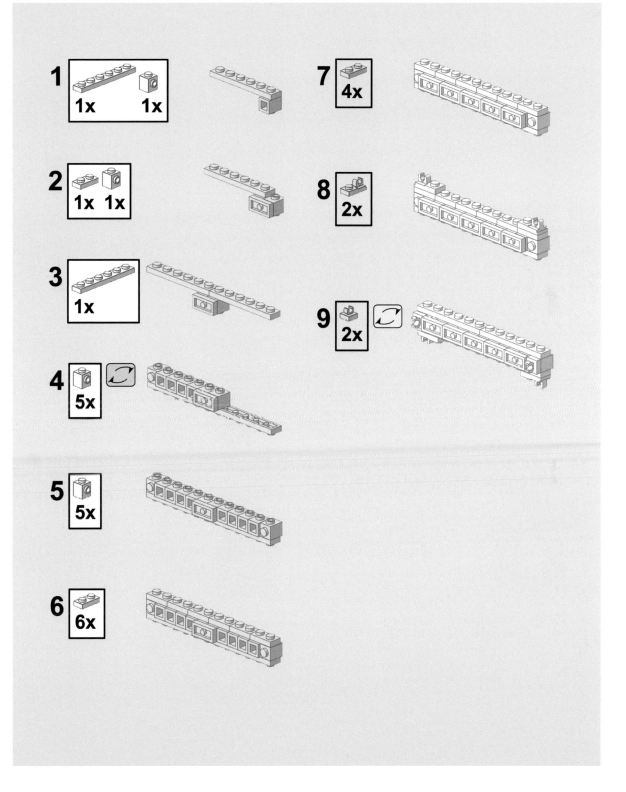

Manhattan Bridge

Completed:
September 2011

Approximate
Number of
LEGO Pieces:
20,800

Dimensions:
138"L × 15"W × 27"H
(350cm × 38cm × 69cm)

Construction of the Manhattan Bridge, connecting Manhattan and Brooklyn, began in 1901. The double-deck bridge is located just north of the Brooklyn Bridge and was designed by Leon Moisseiff. Its lower roadway contains three lanes for vehicles, four tracks for subway lines, a wide pedestrian walkway on the south side, and a bikeway on the north side. The upper roadway, which now comprises four lanes for vehicles, was utilized by streetcars when the bridge first opened.

The opportunity to create my representation of this bridge came about in 2009, when I was asked to participate in an exhibit in New York City. The Manhattan Bridge is one of my favorite structures in the city, and it was celebrating its centenary that year. I was also drawn to the challenge of replicating an exposed-steel-frame structure out of LEGO bricks. To me, the medium lends itself naturally to building in a brick or stone wall fashion. Rendering steel girders was a new challenge, and I was up for it.

My build process for this project did not involve sketching on paper. The first step was to focus on a small detail and let the replication of that detail help determine the proportional size of the overall piece. While this rendering is not nearly to scale, I knew I wanted this bridge to be big. I'm pleased to say that it is almost twelve feet long! The detail I focused on first were the blue Xs in the towers of the bridge. The number of LEGO shapes available in this shade of blue was very limited at the time I built this piece, so part of my development process was to determine what shapes were available in this color. From there I designed the Xs and the rest of the bridge using only those shapes. Once I had those factors finalized, I built a mock-up out of gray pieces that I had on hand. After I was satisfied with my design, I went out and purchased the same pieces in blue and built the final structure.

The model of this bridge utilizes steel armatures embedded in the middle roadway section for support. They are fixed in place with epoxy. Using steel armatures in my work prevents damage in transit and also allows for a quick and stable setup at exhibitions.

I'm assembling the bridge for the photo shoot. It usually takes about one hour to prepare and set up this piece for exhibitions.

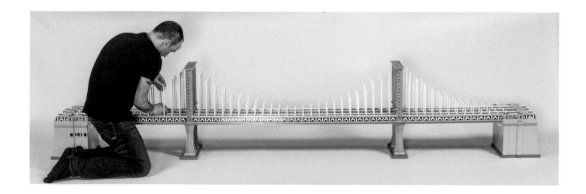

Tower detailing. The presentation here is a balance of color and texture.

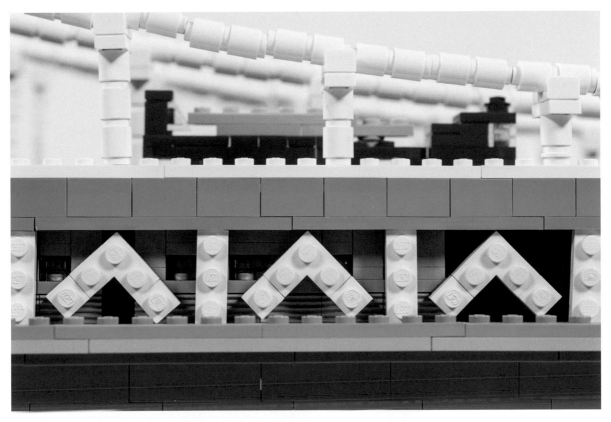

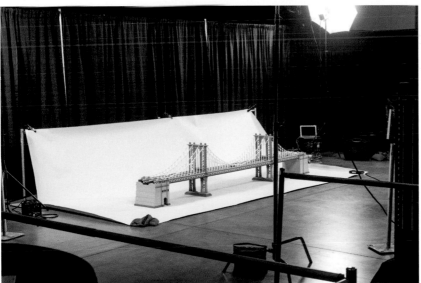

Top: Fire truck racing over the bridge. Note the subway car on the level below it.

Left: A very cool shot of the photo shoot setup for the bridge. Shooting the bridge was a little challenging because of its length.

Tower Base

Working within the established overall size of my bridge, I had to use the studs-facing-out technique to get the effect of the steel tapering out at the bottoms and the tops of the bridge's supports.

Detailing of the footings. I wanted to attain the feel of steel with subtle angles and was able to accomplish this here.

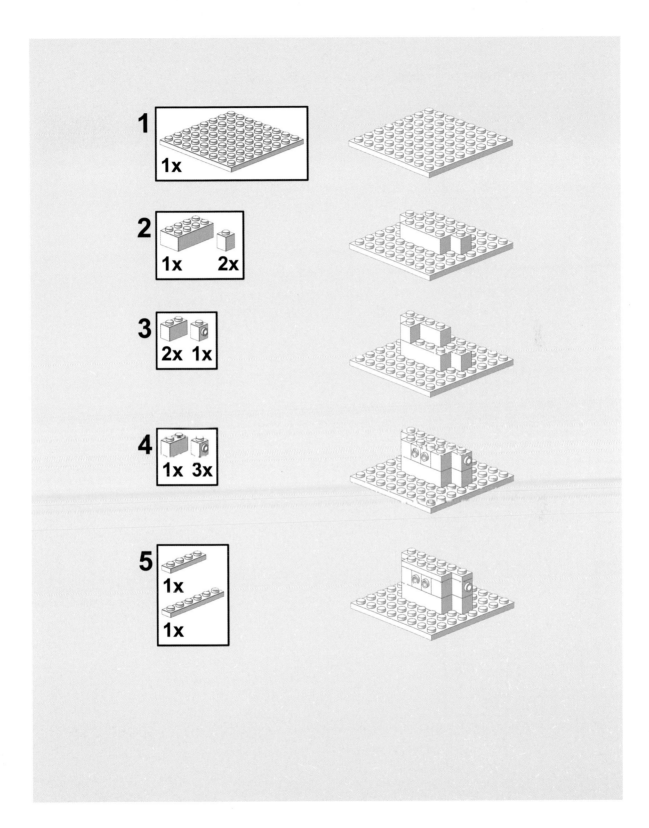

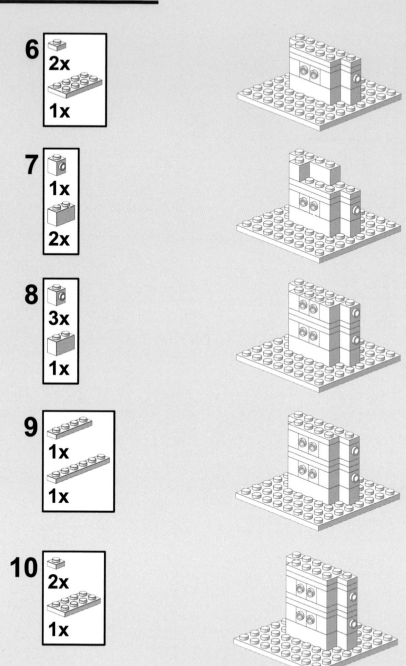

6
2x
1x

7
1x
2x

8
3x
1x

9
1x
1x

10
2x
1x

11

1x
2x

12

3x
1x

13

1 1x 2 1x 1x

x2

1 1x 2 1x 1x

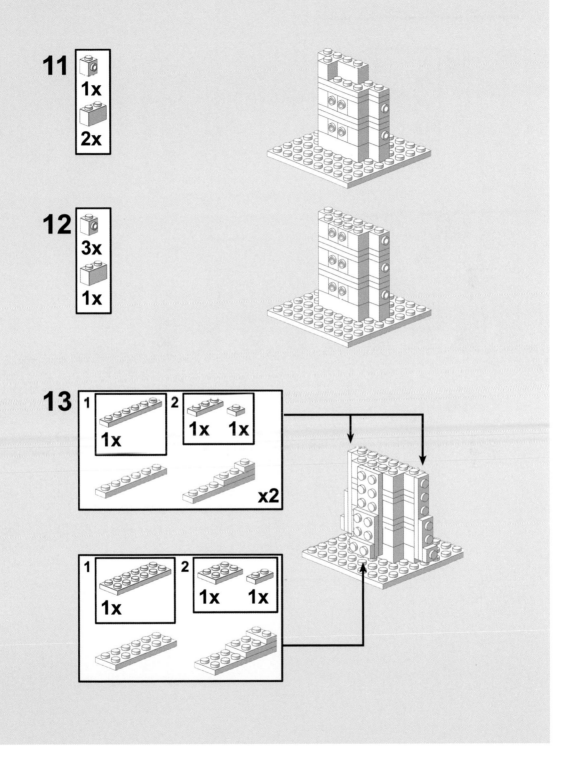

14
2x
1x

15
2x
1x

16
1
1x
1x
2
1x 2x
x5

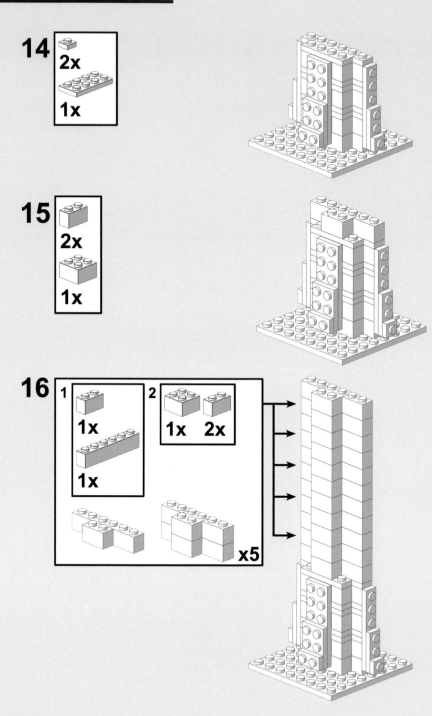

17 2x 1x 1x

18 3x

19 2x

20 1x 2x

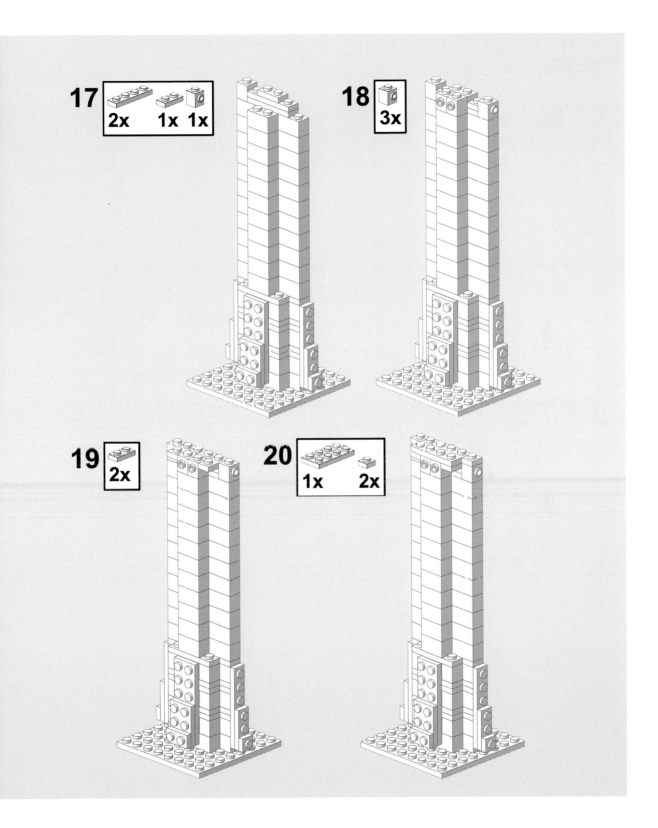

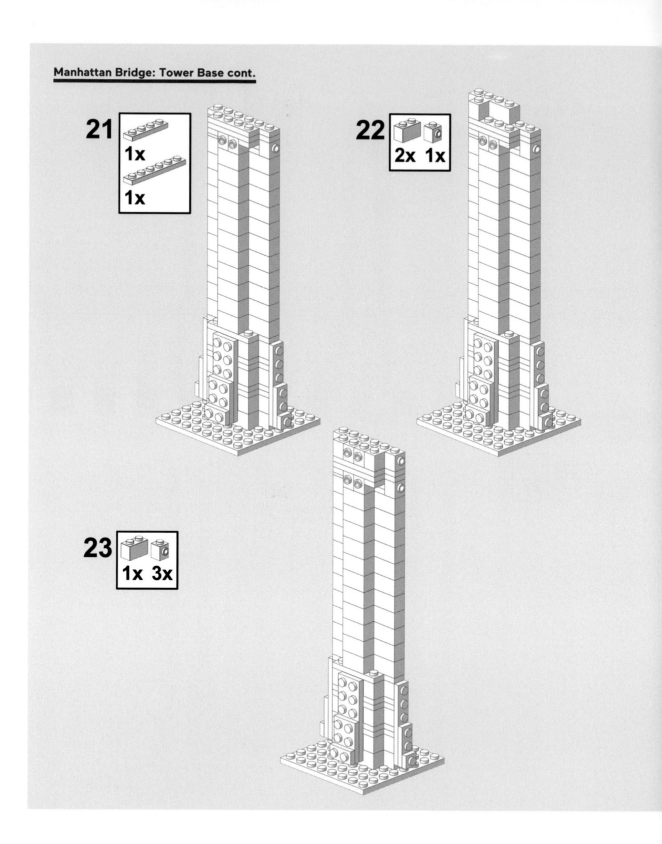

21 1x 1x

22 2x 1x

23 1x 3x

24 1x 2x

25 1x 1x

26 2x 1x

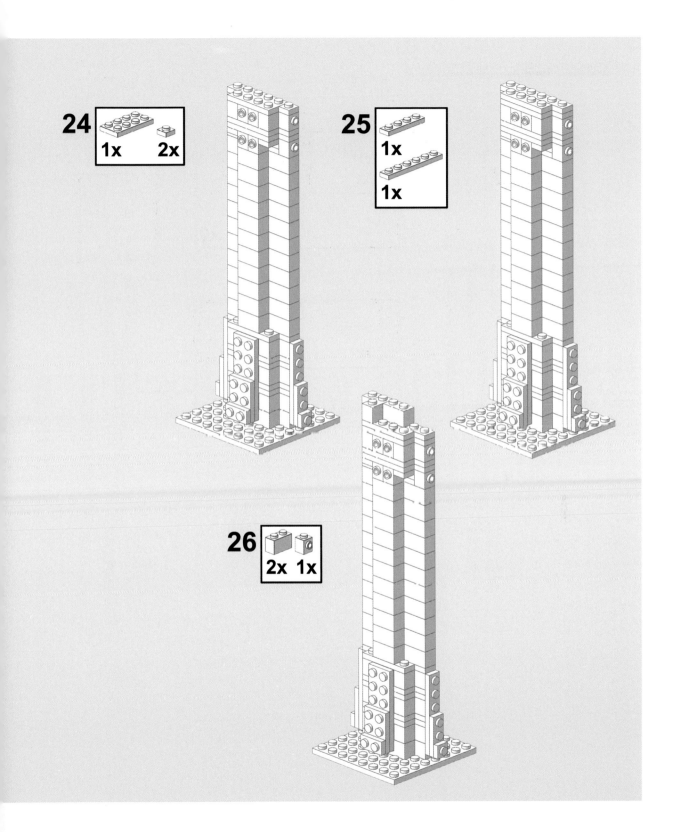

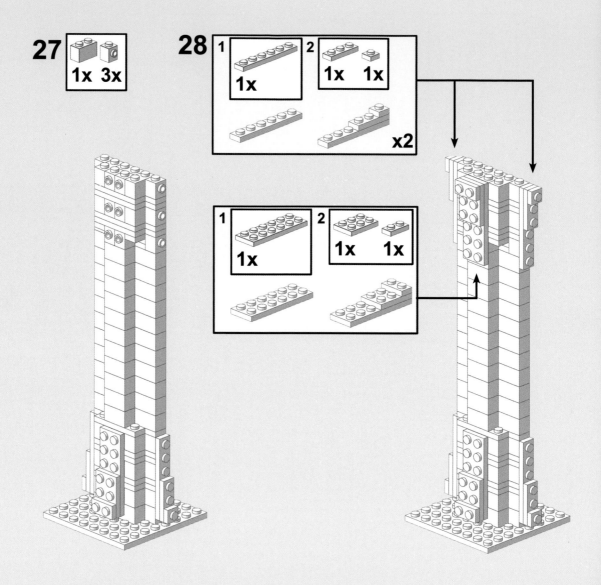

29 1x 1x

30 1x 1x 1x

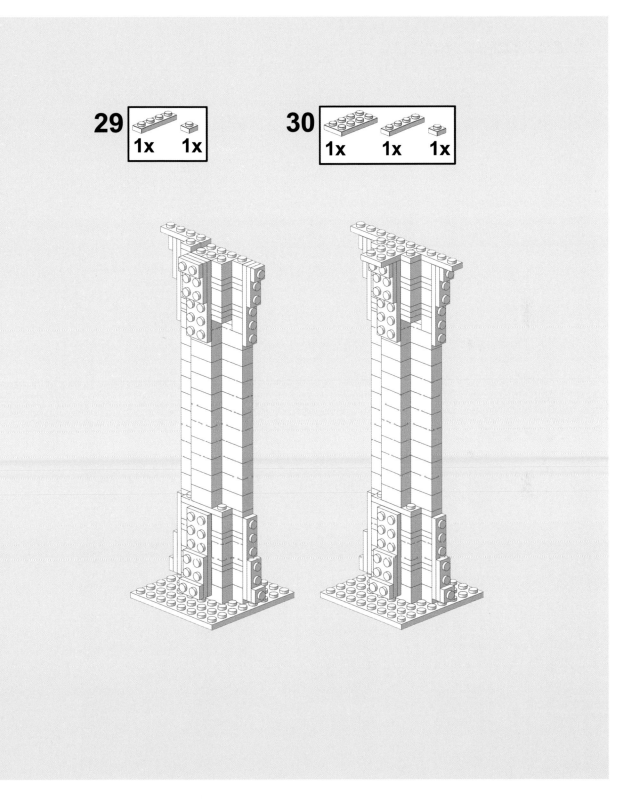

Woolworth Building

Completed:
October 2012

Approximate
Number of
LEGO Pieces:
120,000

Dimensions:
20"L × 29"W × 91"H
(51cm × 74cm × 231cm)

The Woolworth Building, constructed between 1910 and 1912, is located on lower Broadway, across from City Hall Park, in the borough of Manhattan. Designed by architect Cass Gilbert, it was the tallest building in the world upon its completion, and it held that title until 1930. The version I created out of LEGO bricks was designed and built in 2012 to celebrate the building's centenary. There was an exhibit in New York City in which I was participating, and I wanted to make a prominent statement by having my entry be huge. This is the largest piece I've worked on to date.

The first step in developing my Woolworth Building was determining the overall construction technique. The options I had in mind were to build it studs facing up (LEGO pieces simply stacked on one another) or to combine studs-facing-up and studs-facing-out (LEGO pieces facing sideways) methods. Building with studs facing out allows for greater detail.

Below: This image shows the intricate detailing of the street level. Note that the windows are built with the pieces facing sideways, and many of the details are created using studs facing out.

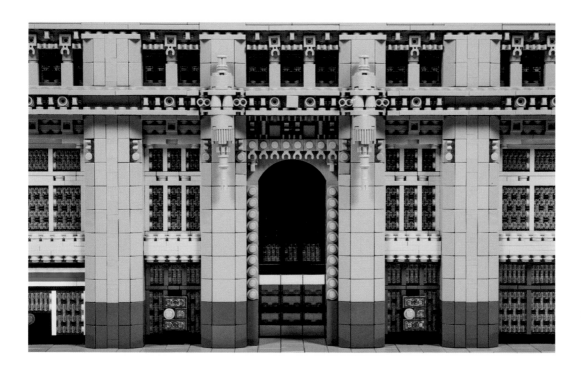

The actual building is designed and built on a steel frame with the facade comprising terra-cotta tile panels, and I wanted to simulate this characteristic in my LEGO version. Ultimately, I designed it using the studs-facing-out building technique, employing tiles as the prominent feature on the facade. This technique allowed me to achieve the slight angles in the facade in a manner that is smooth and not blocky. When working with LEGO bricks, attaining slight curves in a non-blocky method can be difficult, especially when the scale of what you are building is not large.

Once I had the overall construction technique established, I sketched out one line of windows for each of the four sides of the building, using pencil and LEGO graph paper. I did this to assess the space between the windows for visual accuracy and to ensure that the body of my LEGO building would represent the body of the actual building as faithfully as I had envisioned. Doing this also ultimately established the footprint of my model. Once I was satisfied with the proportions of my sketch, I built the footprint using basic 2 × 4 stud LEGO pieces. This allowed me to double-check my sketch proportions and also gave me a physical guide to firmly establish the positioning of the windows and the column areas of the facade.

It took me about two weeks to sort out the process, make a final decision, and be comfortable with my ultimate direction. An additional consideration in my decision-making was what LEGO pieces were available in the colors and the large quantities needed to build this piece. Since the main color was white, I had many options: White is a prominent color in the LEGO parts and color scheme.

Once my design was finalized, I set out to build the approximately twenty-five hundred windows required in this model. Each window is made of eight LEGO pieces and could be built and assembled ahead of the building itself. Once the windows were completed, I started building the model from the sidewalk up.

There are many ornamental details in the Woolworth Building, but replicating them was not all that difficult. Again, since they are white and white is a very common LEGO color, I investigated what LEGO pieces were available and the quantities needed, and then decided on my design approach from there.

The Woolworth Building is the most parts-intensive work I've designed and built to date. It comprises approximately one hundred twenty thousand LEGO pieces and took more than two hundred hours to construct. It was built in eight sections, so it can easily be moved and transported to exhibits and quickly set up for viewing.

Opposite, above:
Looking down at the top of the tower, at an angle.

Opposite, below:
In the ornaments above and around the Broadway-facing entrance.

Above: The back roof section. I used Google Earth to determine the placement of the HVAC units. The roofline, shows the studs-facing-out texture in the green areas and the dormers up close.

Right: This photo shows a close-up of the window design. There are more than twenty-five hundred windows in this building, and most of them were built separately, ahead of the building itself.

Left: Shot showing the street-level detail of the freight entrance door.

Below: Street-level corner shot, showing the details and how they continue around the sides of the building.

Tower

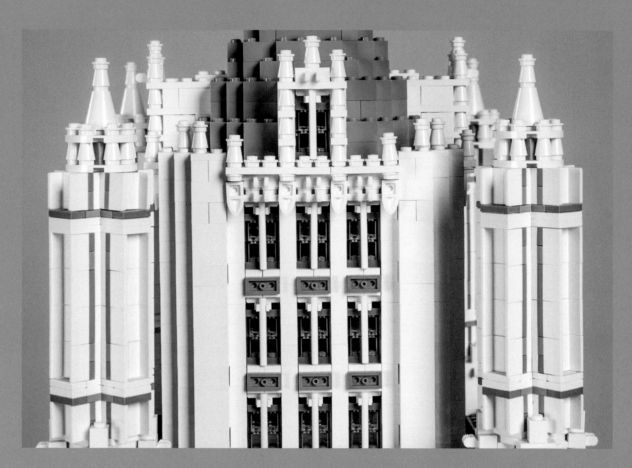

Atop the Woolworth Building
are four ornamental column towers.
These highlight different-colored
tiles and also have some very fine
lines. To render these in LEGO
bricks, I first built 2 × 2 stud inner
columns and then attached panel
pieces to them, topping them
off with two different-size cones.

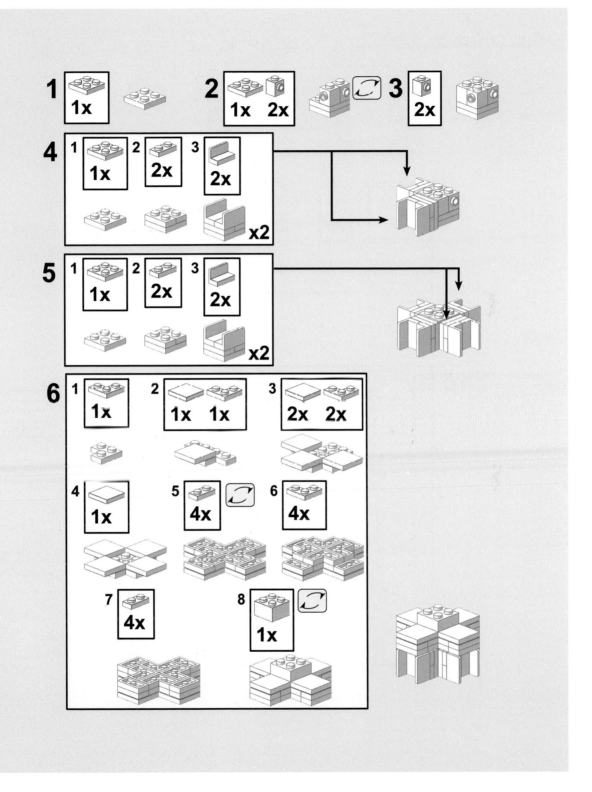

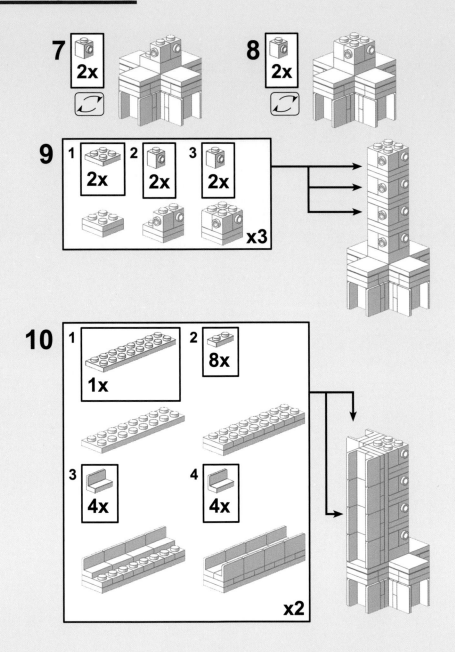

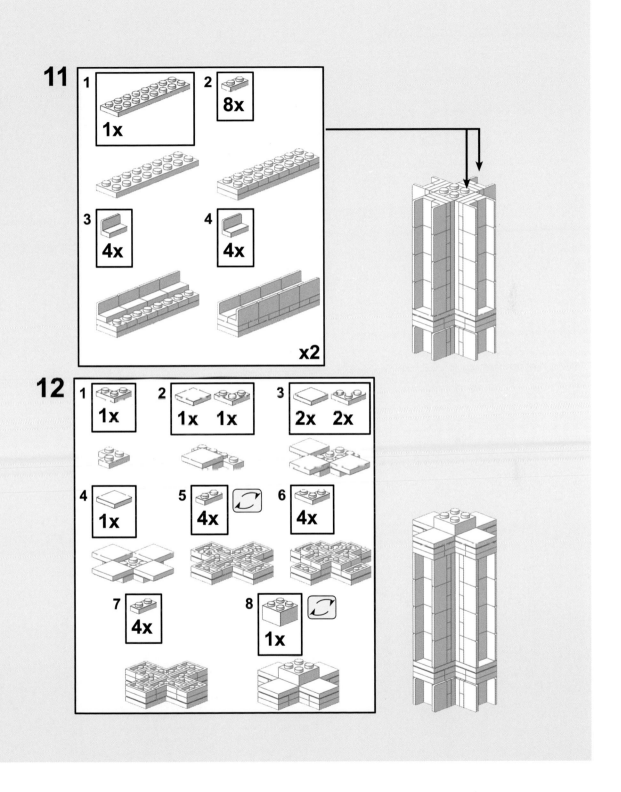

13 2x

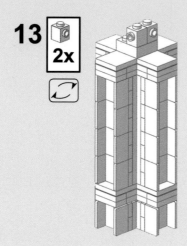

14 2x

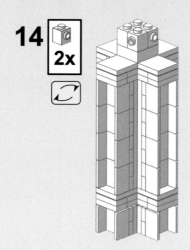

15

1 **1x**
2 **2x**
3 **2x**

x2

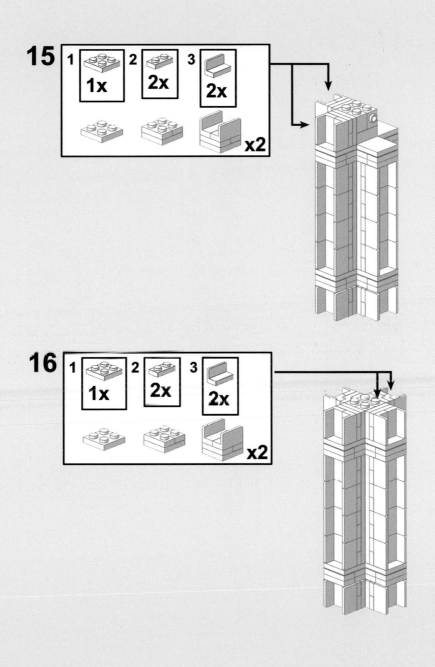

16

1 **1x**
2 **2x**
3 **2x**

x2

17

1x

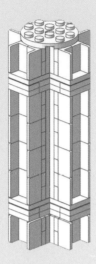

18

8x

1x

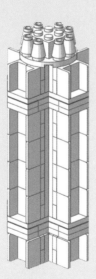

19 1x

20 1x 1x

21 9x

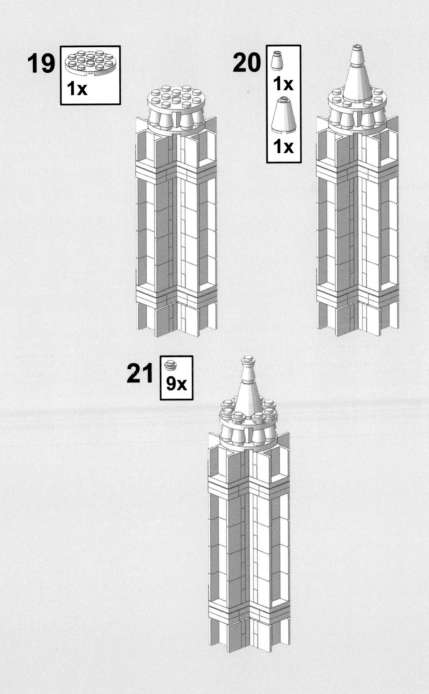

Balcony

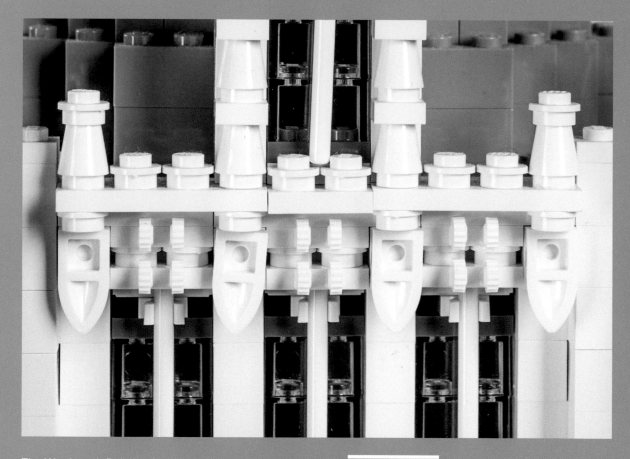

The Woolworth Building is adorned with many details from bottom to top, including the highly detailed balconies. My design for these is simple, using standard plates along with click-hinge plates to elicit more detail.

One of the many balconies. Lots of detail is packed into this very small area.

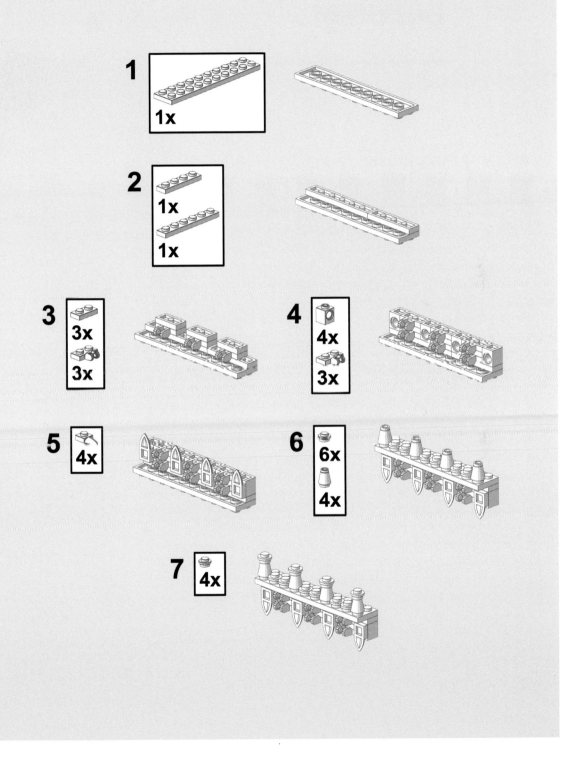

1 1x

2 1x 1x

3 3x 3x

4 4x 3x

5 4x

6 6x 4x

7 4x

Helmsley Building

Completed:
August 2017

Approximate
Number of
LEGO Pieces:
14,700

Dimensions:
22"L × 15"W × 42"H
(56cm × 38cm × 107cm)

The Helmsley Building has long been one of my favorite New York City buildings. It spans an entire block of Park Avenue between East 45th and East 46th Streets. It was designed by Warren and Wetmore, the same firm that designed Grand Central Terminal, which is just to the south. One of the first challenges with my rendering was determining what colors to use. There are a few color combinations that would have been workable. I chose to make my version with tan on the street level and cornice details and dark tan on the overall body of the building. Once I had decided on the color, I went to work designing the footprint of the building. Much as in my building process for other structures, I walked the perimeter of the actual building, taking photographs and noting the placement of doors for the various street-facing shops as well as the entrance to the offices above, to ensure accuracy. For the roof and air-conditioning unit placement, I utilized Google Earth satellite images.

This building has a very large footprint, and because of this I decided to render it in a smaller scale than my Woolworth Building (page 70). Working in a smaller scale is challenging when it comes to replicating details, and it was important to me to maintain as much accuracy as I could: I successfully included more than two thousand windows. The smaller scale dictated that I utilize jumper plates. Jumper plates permit building at half-stud intervals, which allows for refined details, such as the window lines inset by one half-stud from the body of the building. The challenge here is that each window line is a column of pieces straight up the facade. To interlock the columns, I employed more than one thousand jumper plates throughout the interior of the building. Using these jumper plates created a very strong and stable structure, which is important for transport and for public exhibits.

Left: Rooftop HVAC units and cornice details.

Below: The north-facing entrance, where Park Avenue is routed through the building. Note the custom-designed and printed sign: "The Helmsley Building."

Spire

The spire of the Helmsley Building presented challenges both in its design and in its color. Building an object intended to represent something round is not all that easy.

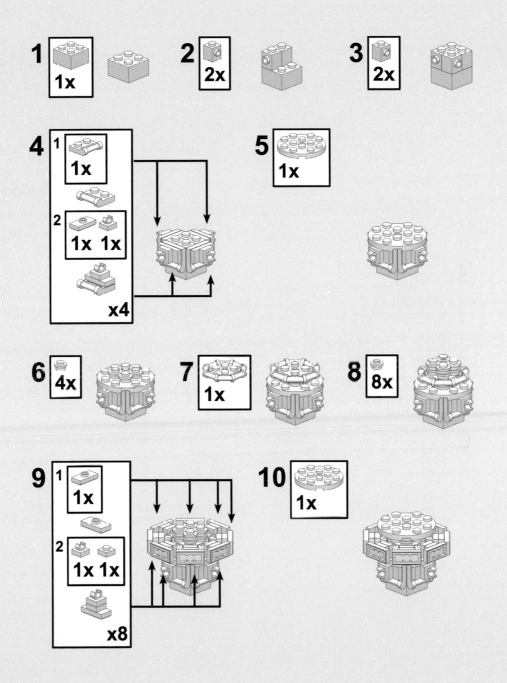

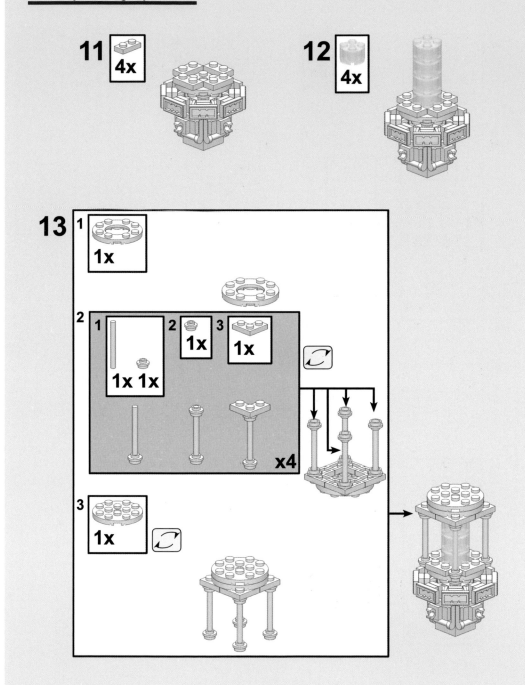

14 4x

15 4x

16 4x 1x 1x

17 1x 1x

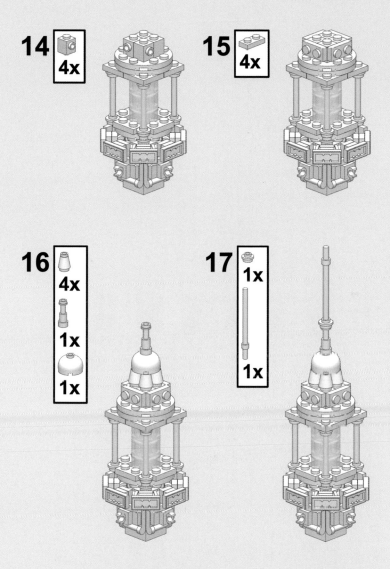

Williamsburgh Savings Bank Tower

Completed:
2009

Approximate
Number of
LEGO Pieces:
5,100

Dimensions:
20"L × 10"W × 46"H
(51cm × 25cm × 117cm)

This piece is the oldest I have chosen to include in this book. The Williamsburgh Savings Bank Tower, now an apartment building known as One Hanson Place, was designed by Halsey, McCormack, and Helmer. It was completed in 1929, and until recently it was the tallest building in Brooklyn. Despite losing that title, it is still one of the borough's most recognizable structures.

The model is significant to me not so much for the building techniques I employed in its creation as for what it represents in my career. It was created for an art exhibit in 2009 and was the first work I exhibited in a gallery (rather than at a LEGO fan convention). This project represents the starting point of my art career and has traveled with me extensively. I lived in full view of this building for fifteen years while residing in Brooklyn, and it was a natural choice for me to re-create it. With the exception of some sideways building techniques on the lower level for the windows, this build utilizes a standard studs-facing-up technique.

Enormous arched windows on street level. Note the different shades of light gray in the facade. I used both the old version of this color as well as the current version.

Clockwise from top: A good shot showing the various step-backs of the building at different rooflines.

Side building entrance and subway entrance.

The different rooflines and top sections.

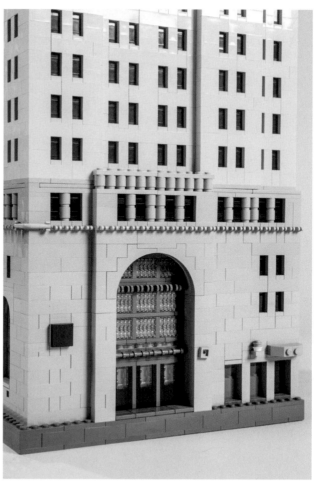

Chrysler Building

Completed:
July 2017

Approximate
Number of
LEGO Pieces:
13,800

Dimensions:
16"L × 16"W × 64"H
(41cm × 41cm × 163cm)

Completed in 1930, the landmark Chrysler Building briefly held the title of the world's tallest building; it was surpassed by the Empire State Building in 1931. With its Art Deco styling and steel facade at the top, this William van Alen–designed building stands prominently in the New York City skyline. It is perhaps the second most recognizable skyscraper in Midtown Manhattan.

To render this icon in LEGO bricks, the two main challenges I faced were determining the palette and then determining the scale. To my eye, and in my recollection of the Chrysler Building in historical black-and-white photos, its facade was gray. But with more research, I discovered that the gray that I thought the building was leans toward a very light gray, if not white. This helped me with my palette decisions. I chose to replicate the steel portion toward the top of this building in the LEGO color light gray, the architectural accents in dark gray, and the body in white, ensuring that there was contrast and separation of the colors and building sections.

When determining the size of my LEGO Chrysler Building, I chose a reduced scale compared to the scale of my Woolworth Building (page 70). I tend to consider scale as it pertains to the medium of LEGO bricks to be the widths of the windows. As a result, while my Woolworth Building has two-stud-wide windows, I created my Chrysler Building with one-stud-wide windows. This was done in an effort to challenge myself in rendering the fine details of a skyscraper in a smaller size.

Street level.
I added flower boxes
to the side
of the entrance of
the building to
add a little splash
of color to an
otherwise monotone
structure.

Opposite: Often times when re-creating existing buildings, I discover things about them that I didn't know previously, like the angled backside of this building, which is shown in the photo.

Neighbor-
hoods

While New York City has an amazing skyline, it is also home to countless low-rise neighborhoods. These typically have their own distinct feel and flavor that is passed down from generation to generation and then absorbed by people who move in. I was lucky to have lived in a number of neighborhoods in Manhattan, the Bronx, and Queens before finally settling in Boerum Hill, Brooklyn.

When I first moved to Boerum Hill, the area was in the very early stages of a renaissance, and there was still a certain level of grittiness to the neighborhood. During the time I was there, it became a sought-after and artistic place to live, bustling with galleries, boutiques, and restaurants. I was greatly inspired by the neighborhood and appreciated the architecture of the buildings. I've enjoyed building them for years. This chapter shares a few types of these low-rise buildings, several in Boerum Hill and some in Manhattan.

Delmonico's

Completed:
March 2018

Approximate
Number of
LEGO Pieces:
6,600

Dimensions:
20"L × 25"W × 20"H
(51cm × 63cm × 51cm)

The restaurant Delmonico's is in a triangle-shaped building at the corner of Beaver and South William Streets in Lower Manhattan. It dates from the 1800s, and a number of neighboring buildings on South William Street are from the same era. Because of its beauty, this building is a frequent subject for New York City photographers. To me and my eye, the building evokes a sense of warmth and soul that is most evident at dusk.

It was an easy choice to include Delmonico's in this book, and aside from the footprint it was a rather straightforward building to replicate. A few unique design features of the building are the large arched windows toward the top and the street-level window awnings. The curvature at the front entrance to the building was another challenge to take on. The piece that makes this curve possible is the hinge plate, and I used many hinge plates in this section. Also of note are the details on the roof—the planters and deck. These were a nice surprise when I reviewed satellite photos of the actual building.

Rooftop details, including the plantings and gardens.

Top: Side view shot showing the warm-toned brick colors used in this piece.

Bottom: Full side shot showing the huge arched windows that help define this building.

Opposite: The entrance of the restaurant.

Awnings

These simple awnings add both style
and texture to this piece. Awnings
would typically not be textured,
but given the smooth sides of the
building and the smooth sidewalk,
I felt the texture added a pleasing
artistic contrast.

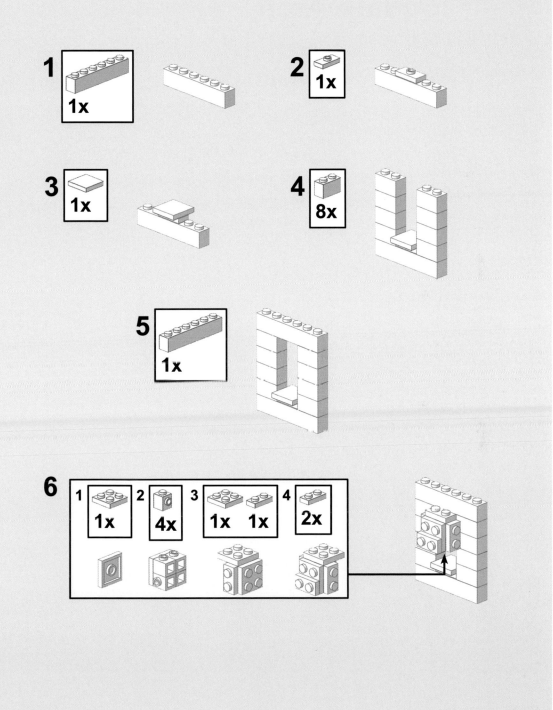

Washington Square Arch

Completed:
April 2018

Approximate
Number of
LEGO Pieces:
2,600

Dimensions:
26"L × 14"W × 9"H
(66cm × 36cm × 23cm)

Washington Square Arch sits at the southernmost point of 5th Avenue and serves as the northern entrance to Washington Square Park, which is itself the gateway to Greenwich Village and New York University. This park has filled many roles during its time, but since the 1960s it has functioned as a gathering place for music, cultural events, and protests.

The two factors that determined the size of this piece were that I wanted to use LEGO minifigures as the statues and I wanted to reproduce the tile paneling on the ceiling inside the arch. Both were achievable in a small size, though replicating details effectively in a small size is a challenge. It was also important to me to include the contrast between the concrete sidewalks and the variously sized paving stones. Achieving this was parts-intensive. Finally, to give the overall piece a stronger presentation and context, I included an expanded area that contains gardens, trees, and wrought-iron fencing.

Left: Overhead side shot facing east that highlights the gardens and landscaping.

Below: Note the undersides of the plates giving a nice texture to the ceiling of the arch.

Opposite: Note the minifigures used as statues here.

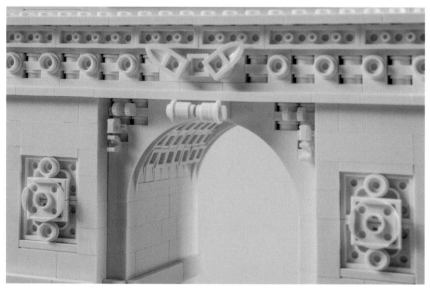

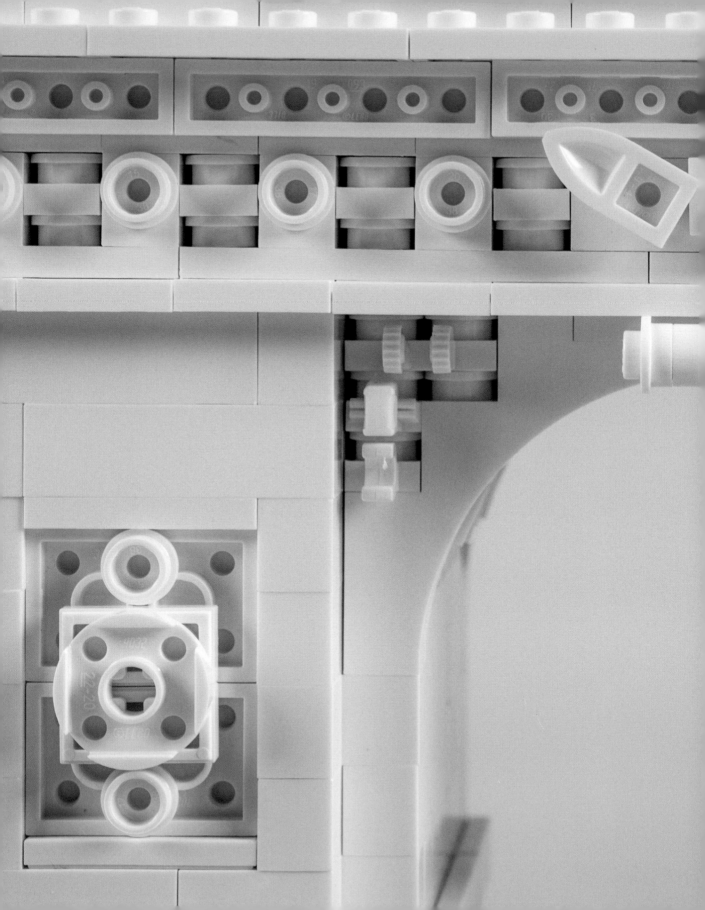

Atlantic
Avenue

Completed:
October 2013

Approximate
Number of
LEGO Pieces:
1,600

Dimensions:
18"L × 11"W × 9"H
(46cm × 28cm × 23cm)

Atlantic Avenue stretches more than ten miles, from the East River all the way to Jamaica, Queens. It also runs right through Boerum Hill. I lived on a block of Atlantic Avenue for a number of years and loved the shops, galleries, restaurants, and bars that occupied the street level. Above those establishments were apartments and homes. This piece represents a common scene on the blocks of Atlantic Avenue in my former neighborhood.

These four buildings are built together as one piece. The coloring of the facades was a very important aspect. I used the current version of brown, a discontinued version of brown, and dark red. These colors are key to evoking the overall feeling and soul of the buildings and blocks this model was made to represent. I varied the storefronts at street level, utilizing the sideways building technique for some of them. Details that bring vitality to this piece are the trees, light poles, and mailboxes on the corner, in addition to the slightly different cornices of each building.

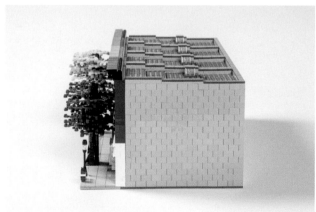

Previous page: Full frontal shot. Note the very slight differences in the colors of the facades. There are two different shades of brown. One is the older version of the color, and the other the current version.

Left, top: Note the different gray colors employed in the wall. Both the older version and the current version of gray are used to provide a weathered effect.

Left, bottom: Side shot shows the roofline gently angling downward toward the backs of the buildings.

Left: Bay windows and two doors. One door is to the street-level shop, and the other door would lead to the apartments on the second and third floors.

Below: Mailboxes on the corner.

Streetlight

This is how I constructed a simple streetlight. Note that the antenna is used upside down.

1

1x 1x

2

1x 1x

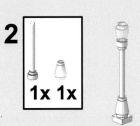

3

1x

1x

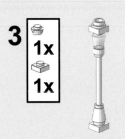

Cornice

Cornices are one of my favorite parts
of buildings. This one is designed
using plates, round plates, and click-
hinge elements for added details.

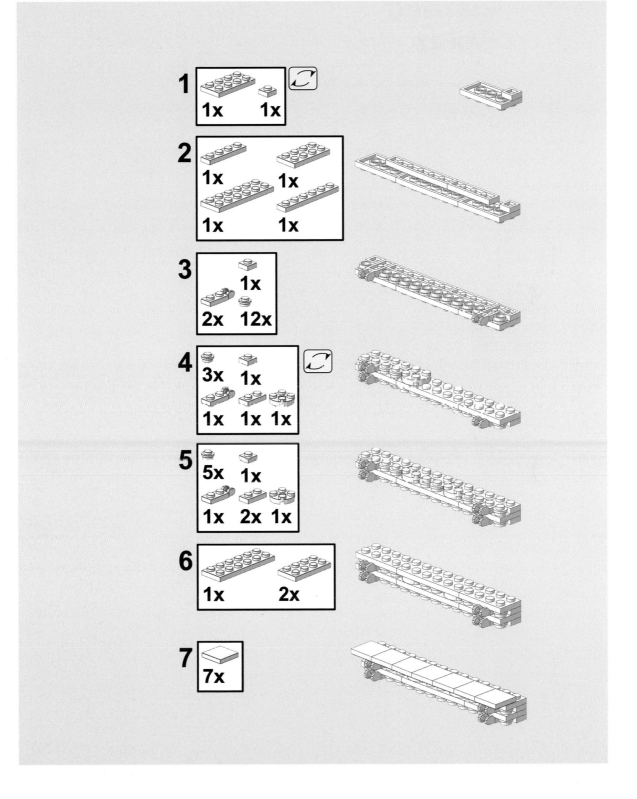

Garden
Shop

Completed:
October 2012

Approximate
Number of
LEGO Pieces:
800

Dimensions:
**5"L × 11"W × 9"H
(13cm × 28cm × 23cm)**

This piece represents a building on Atlantic Avenue in Boerum Hill—a typical architectural design on a good number of blocks in that neighborhood. In structure and style it is quite similar to some of my other works, but in this model I introduced some unique aesthetics, parts usage, and building techniques.

In an effort to add some curvature to the cornice, I used 1 × 4 stud LEGO arch pieces. The drawback with these is that I could not fill in the arch gap and had to inset the wall behind the arch. Represented in this facade is the change in the coloring of light gray pieces from the older, warmer light gray to the newer, colder light gray with a slight bluish tint. Here I've mixed the two grays to achieve a weathered effect, which is enhanced by the mixing in of some dark orange pieces.

On the side of the building I used a different technique to achieve a look of weathered exposed brick. It is a simple method, in which I built a section of the wall with the studs facing sideways. Then I covered the studs with tiles in a brick-like pattern. Last, for the lintels above the windows I ventured beyond the more standard LEGO shapes I tend to use in my work and employed a more specialized piece. I think it fits quite well as a lintel and am happy with the appearance.

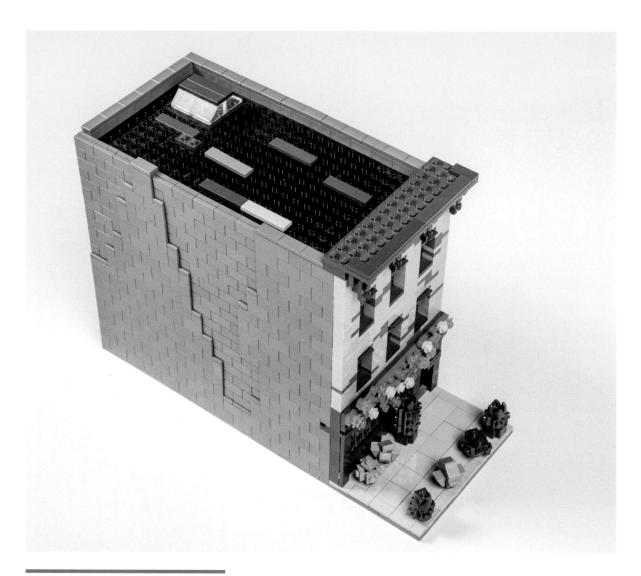

This is an excellent shot of the facade
and the left side of the building,
showing the weathering effects on
both. Note the different textures and
colors used on the sides to achieve
these results. The rooftop elements
include a few random boards and a
skylight. Many Brooklyn buildings have
skylights on their roofs. Also note
the two different shades of brown
in the cornice at the front of the roof.
I used them deliberately to elicit
a weathered effect.

Above: There is a lot going on in this shot. Note the brown specialty piece used above each window. The facade is constructed of plates, which give a brick-like appearance. This piece is also a good showcase of the older gray color mixed with the newer gray color. The full weathering effect was achieved by randomly interspersing dark orange plates in the facade.

Left: Bushes and trees for sale on the sidewalk in front of the shop.

Cornice

I wanted to achieve the effect of an arch within a cornice on this building. Adding the drop-down click hinges with studs facing outward was also a key element that helped establish some depth and texture.

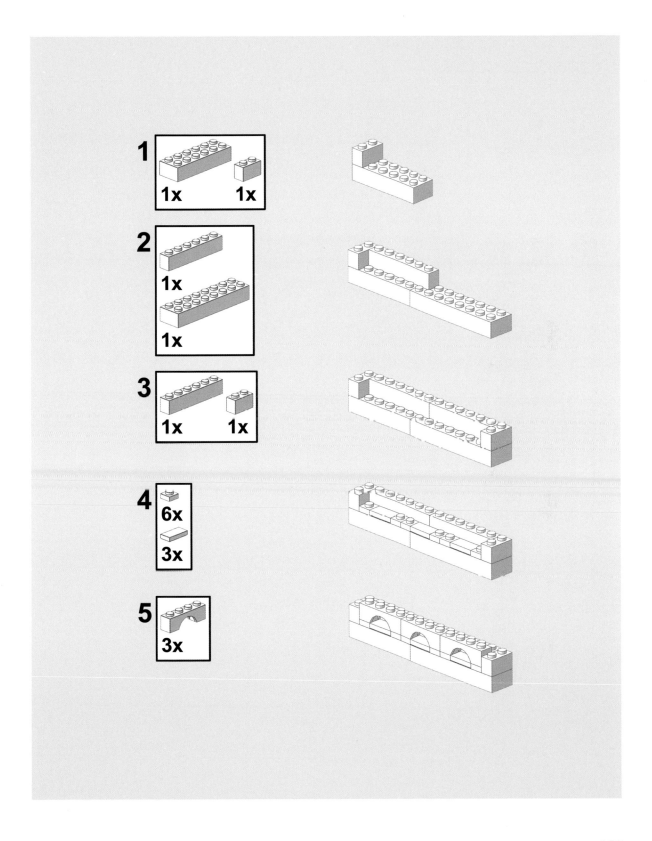

1 1x 1x

2 1x 1x

3 1x 1x

4 6x 3x

5 3x

6 3x

7 2x
2x

8 2x
1x

9 1x
3x

10 6x

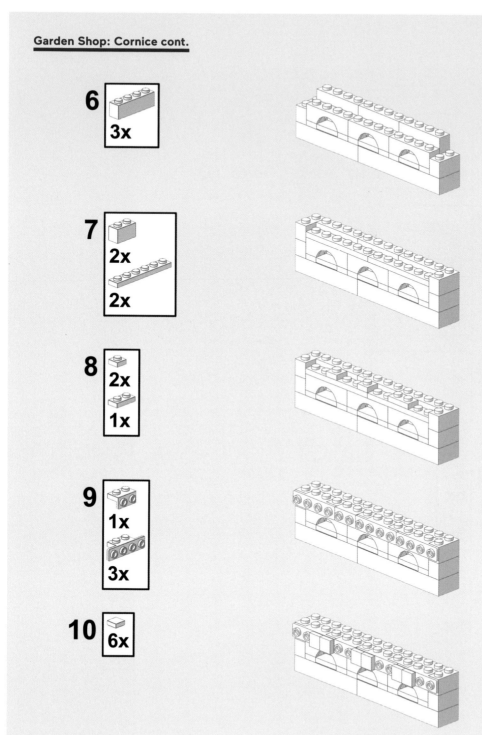

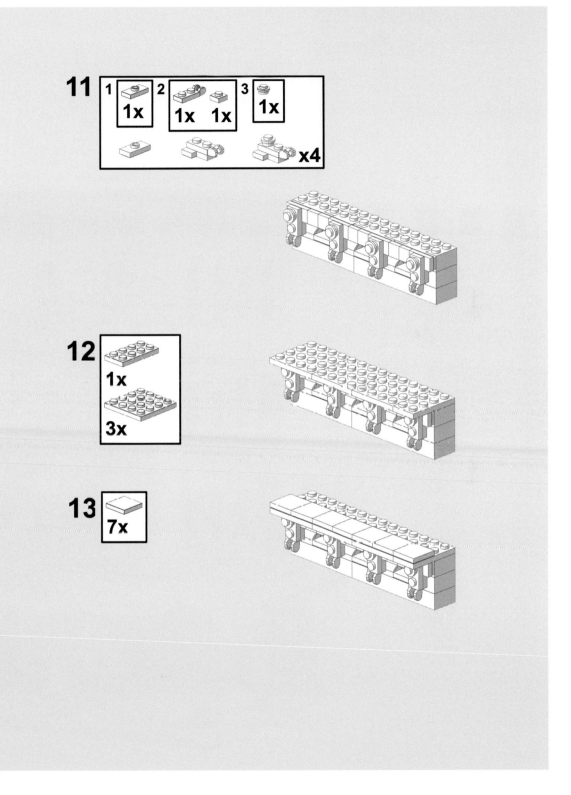

Building
on Bond

Completed:
May 2013

Approximate
Number of
LEGO Pieces:
1,800

Dimensions:
9"L × 21"W × 11"H
(23cm × 53cm × 28cm)

Building on Bond is a restaurant located in a four-story building that occupies the corner of Bond and Pacific Streets in Boerum Hill, Brooklyn. I lived around the corner from this building for fifteen years, so I walked by it frequently. I was drawn to the sidewalk tables and the vibrant energy that emanated from the restaurant. This is one of the aspects of an urban neighborhood that I gravitate toward.

Designing this piece was a fun exercise in working with colors that were not all that common at the time. The sand-green awnings, the olive-green street-level walls, and the medium-dark flesh-colored body of the building are brought together by the brown-and-green trees. The fire escapes and the corner details on the facade bring even more vibrancy to this work.

Opposite, top:
Street-level entrance. I balanced the various shades of green with the contrasting earth tones.

Opposite, bottom:
Stained glass window. On the inside, behind this stained-glass window, is the internal staircase to the different floors of the building.

Right:
Fire escape.

Windows

In this piece a unique building
technique is used to create
the restaurant windows on the
street level. They're built sideways,
with the studs facing to the side
rather than upward. This technique
allows for narrow detail on the
windowpanes.

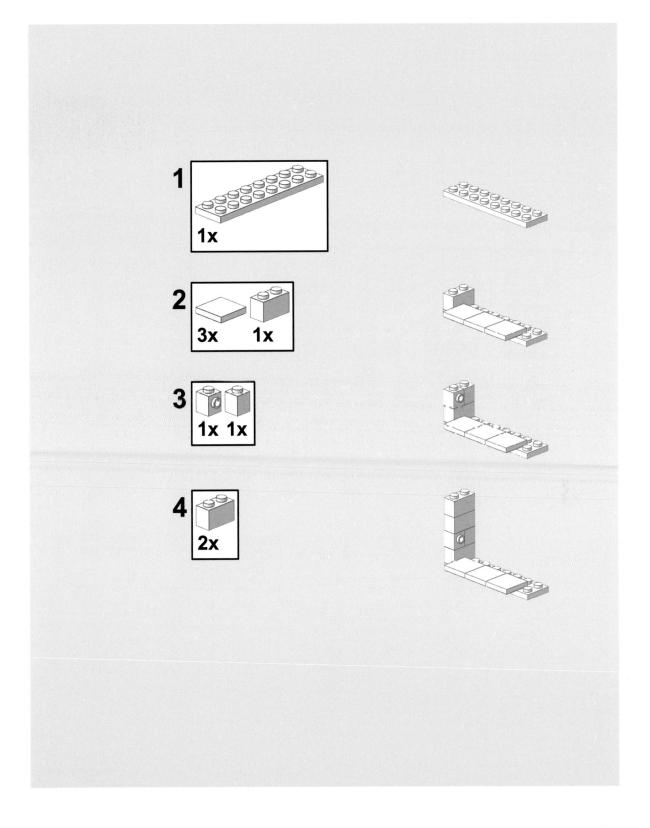

1 1x

2 3x 1x

3 1x 1x

4 2x

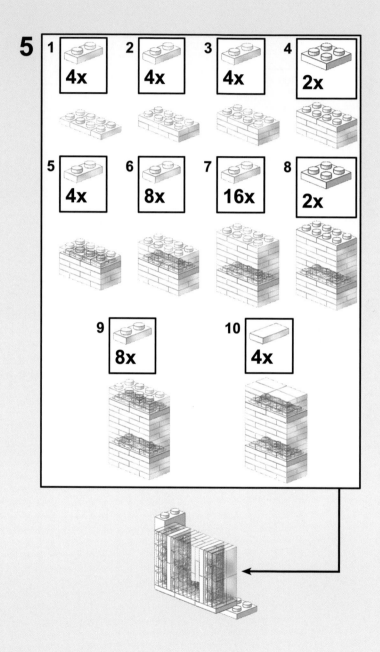

6

4x

7

1x

8

2x

1x

9

1x

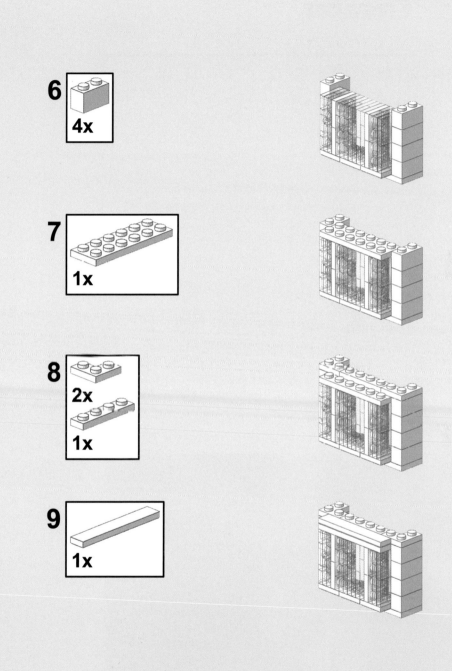

Apollo
Theater

| Completed:
December 2017 | Approximate
Number of
LEGO Pieces:
1,400 | Dimensions:
**9"L × 20"W × 17"H
(23cm × 51cm × 43cm)** |

The Apollo Theater has a place in my heart for a number of reasons. Since I'm a musician, the historical significance of the Apollo Theater is important to me. Many musical acts that I grew up listening to either originated in New York City or gave key performances at the Apollo Theater. I also played softball in New York for twelve years, and one of the sets of softball fields we played at regularly was in Harlem. I'd pass the Apollo each night on my walk there.

Because of the size of this piece, I knew I'd want to employ custom-printed pieces, as I did with Junior's restaurant (page 148). Without the custom printing, this piece would not present as I felt it needed to, and I am more than happy to stretch the limits of working with LEGO as a medium by including custom-printed elements.

I had a lot of fun designing the marquee and the tower that houses the tall signage. I chose the LEGO color dark azure to represent the neon marquee lights and added the custom-printed **AMATEUR NIGHT** signage.

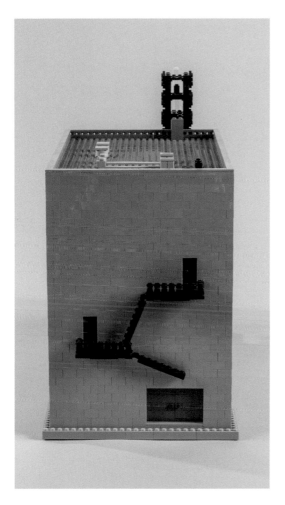

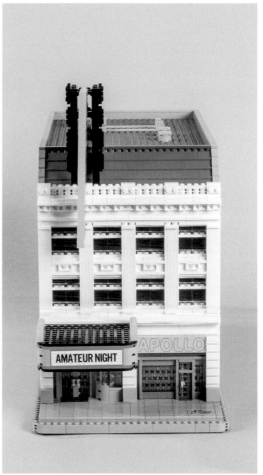

Opposite: Upright signage. This was a little tricky to make stable. It is a bit fragile.

Above, left: Back of the building showing stage doors and fire escapes.

Above, right: Straight frontal shot showing facade details. Note the cornice details with the bottoms of the LEGO pieces exposed.

Junior's Restaurant (Brooklyn)

Completed: **November 2017**	Approximate Number of LEGO Pieces: **1,500**	Dimensions: **19"L × 17"W × 9"H** **(48cm × 43cm × 23cm)**

Junior's restaurant in Downtown Brooklyn was a fun build for me. It has an interestingly shaped footprint, which I used LEGO hinge plates to achieve, and it also epitomizes the low-rise commercial architecture that I really like. I decided to use an older version of the building as my prototype. The current building, which was renovated in the 1980s, lacks much of the detail and soul that the earlier version had.

This rendering also gave me an opportunity to utilize custom-printed LEGO pieces. Tommy and Elaine Armstrong, from the Original BrickEngraver in North Carolina, have supplied me with my printed and engraved pieces for a good number of years. I commissioned a fellow artist named Rusty von Dyl, of Von Dyl Design in San Diego, California, to create the art and graphics to print. But before any printing could take place, I had to make the building and also the sections that would be printed. Sizing was important, so I built mock-ups and worked with Rusty to ensure the graphics were the right size. Then I sent the mock-ups, along with the art files, to Tommy and Elaine to print for me. Without the printed elements, Junior's would not have the vibrancy and soul that it has. I used the printed elements in much the same way I employ trees and plants: to bring a piece to life.

The angled corner entrance to Junior's.

3.

Fire-

houses

In the late 1990s, while I was living in Manhattan and the Bronx and exploring the city, I began to take note of the varying architectural styles of the firehouses of the New York City Fire Department (FDNY). I started to appreciate their individual characteristics and learned how to assess their ages based on their architecture. Some are just a few years old, while others are more than one hundred. Each has features and nuances that are unique to its era. Since this discovery, I regularly design and build firehouses from various cities. This section presents a walk-through of a series of FDNY firehouses whose architecture spans the years.

Manhattan: Engine 33/Ladder 9

Completed:	Approximate	Dimensions:
June 2017	Number of	**16"L × 11"W × 15"H**
	LEGO Pieces:	**(41cm × 28cm × 38cm)**
	1,600	

The Engine Company 33 and Ladder Company 9 firehouse, on Great Jones Street in Manhattan's East Village, is one of my favorites. Its arch is magnificent and its cornice is intricately detailed. The firehouse, which is still in active use, was completed in 1899 and is now listed on the National Register of Historic Places.

When designing my projects, I'll often gravitate to a detail that I want to render with some degree of accuracy and build out from there. In the case of this firehouse, that detail was the arch and the windows beneath it. The rest followed rather easily. I constructed the body of this rendering using bricks in the LEGO color sand red, which at the time of this build was quite rare. Pots with plants and flowers near the doors are details that I enjoy including in my work and that add a nice pop of color, contrasting with a building's typically muted earth tone. I also incorporated a custom-designed and custom-printed September 11 memorial plaque on the lower section between the bay doors.

Street-level details. Note the planters between the bays. Also of significance are the garage doors. I stacked the bricks with-out interlocking them to give the impression of paneling. Also of note is the custom designed and printed 9/11 memorial plaque beneath the light.

Brooklyn: Engine 224

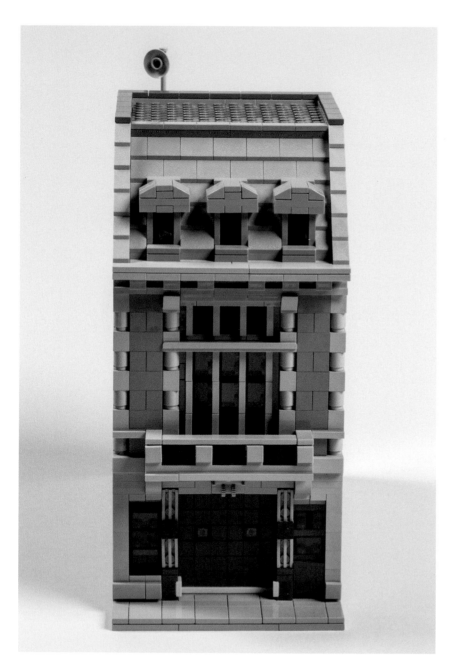

Opposite, left: Rooftop communication tower.

Opposite, right: Street-level details. Note the yellow safety stripe toward the bottom of the garage door along with the yellow safety guides to the lower right and left of the door. These assist the firefighters when they are backing the fire truck into the station.

Completed:
March 2014

Approximate
Number of
LEGO Pieces:
600

Dimensions:
5"L × 10"W × 10"H
(13cm × 25cm × 25cm)

Engine Company 224, on Hicks Street in Brooklyn Heights, calls this firehouse home. This Renaissance Revival–style building was finished in 1903, a number of years after the majority of buildings around it were completed.

The prototype building is packed with details. When rendering in a much smaller scale, one has to select what details to include and decide whether additional details, within size and LEGO limitations, can be added to complement the building and make the model appear more detailed even if, in fact, the actual building isn't. Some of the details around the garage door in this model do not exist in the real building, but I feel they add a nice touch to my rendering. One of the challenges with this piece was the dormers on the roof. These were designed sideways, with the studs facing the side rather than upward. Details like the yellow striping toward the bottom of the bay door add both realism and some nice visual contrast.

Dormers

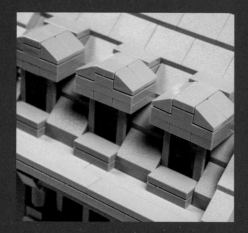

The dormers on this building were a bit tricky to build. The small size of the parts, and their limited availability in the color I used, presented challenges. There is a lot happening on the inside to make the dormers work, that cannot be seen from the outside.

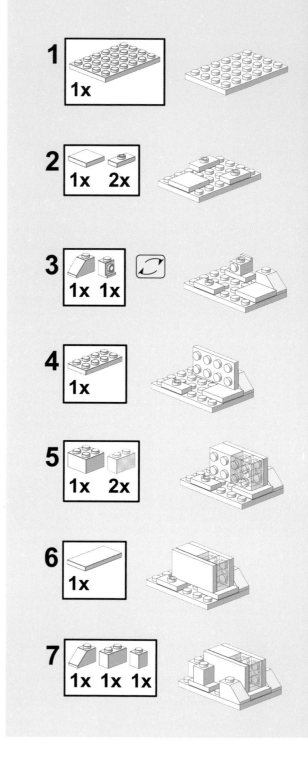

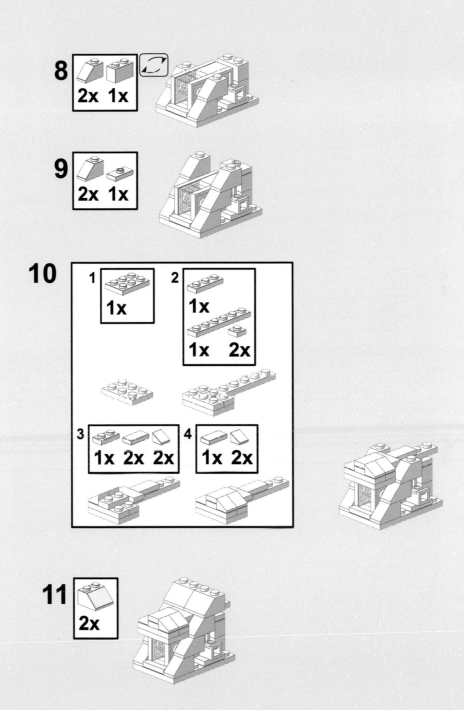

Brooklyn:
Engine 226

Completed: **September 2012**	Approximate Number of LEGO Pieces: **650**	Dimensions: **5"L × 10"W × 8"H** **(13cm × 25cm × 20cm)**

Brooklyn's Engine Company 226 serves the neighborhood of Boerum Hill, near Downtown Brooklyn. The firehouse sits on a mostly residential tree-lined block of State Street, which runs parallel to the heavily trafficked Atlantic Avenue.

One of the unique aspects of this design is the five-stud-wide garage door entrance. When building with LEGO pieces, I find that even-numbered stud widths make for easier constructions. In the case of this building, however, the windows on the second floor would not have aligned to my liking had I worked with a six-stud-wide garage door, so I reduced it to five studs and had to carefully engineer other aspects of the facade to make everything work together properly. Details are key to my work, so on the second floor we have a window air conditioner.

Street level.
Note that the
garage door
is constructed
with LEGO plates.
This was done
to suggest the
ribbing effect
of large metal
garage doors.

Bronx: Engine 63/ Ladder 39, Battalion 15

Completed: **June 2014**	Approximate Number of LEGO Pieces: **1,100**	Dimensions: **14"L × 16"W × 12"H** **(36cm × 41cm × 30cm)**

This model represents one of the FDNY's more recently built firehouses. It is located on 233rd Street in the Bronx and houses Engine Company 63 and Ladder Company 39 of Battalion 15. The firehouse was completed in 2013, replacing two older firehouses that had each housed one company.

A notable feature of this firehouse is that the designers retained a section of the previous firehouse that was home to Engine 63, to the right rear. I've included this section in my work too. It's worth pointing out that, to the left of my piece, I utilized a sideways building technique. In a rendering this size, this technique allows for the thinner upward-ribbing detail that was needed.

For the roof I used a discontinued dark gray. The earthy color provides just the right amount of contrast with the facade color.

Left: Fire hydrant, trees, and side entrance.

Opposite, below: I sourced the engraved and printed bricks from the Original BrickEngraver in North Carolina. The FDNY sign is brick built, totally out of LEGO.

Bronx: Rescue 3 (Then)

Completed:	Approximate Number of LEGO Pieces:	Dimensions:
November 2017	**1,100**	**11"L × 16"W × 11"H** **(28cm × 41cm × 28cm)**

Bronx: Rescue 3 (Now)

Completed:	Approximate Number of LEGO Pieces:	Dimensions:
November 2017	**1,900**	**19"L × 21"W × 9"H** **(48cm × 53cm × 23cm)**

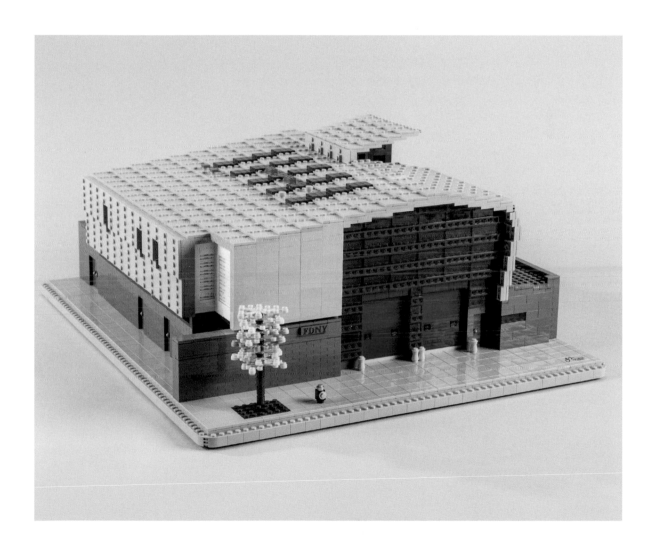

These works are then-and-now representations of Rescue Company 3, from the Bronx. I developed and built these two pieces at the same time, but they are clearly based on prototypes from different eras. They present strikingly different architectural styles, each indicative of the time in which the building was constructed.

When I was designing the earlier firehouse, my first challenge was selecting colors. As happens frequently, the availability of parts in particular colors affected my creative decision-making. I chose to build the facade in the LEGO colors brown, medium-dark flesh, and tan. The LEGO color dark tan might have worked where I wanted to use medium-dark flesh, and there are more pieces and shapes available in dark tan. But I focused on color over piece availability. This limited my choices of details and features to replicate and also challenged me to consider a different approach to reproducing these details. The very textured facade of the building is one example. I used plates to achieve the brick-like texture and then used tiles, with their little indented bottom grooves, to represent a linear textural detail that existed in the prototype. The bay doors are custom-printed sections that were sourced through Von Dyl Design and the Original BrickEngraver.

An aspect of the new firehouse that intrigued me is its aluminum facade. I decided that the position of the seams between each LEGO piece was important to me, so I avoided interlocking the pieces on the front facade and simply stacked them instead. This was done in an effort to minimize a brick-like appearance on the facade and, I hoped, enhance the appearance of sheet metal. On the lower level of the building, however, I *did* want the pieces to give a brick-like appearance and I *did* interlock them. These two different approaches show the significance texture has for me when working with LEGO bricks. For an additional texture, on the side and roof I used exposed studs to delineate the effect of the metal ribbing that is apparent in these areas of the actual building. I could have used LEGO pieces from the tile family here, but it matters to me to have some exposed studs in my work.

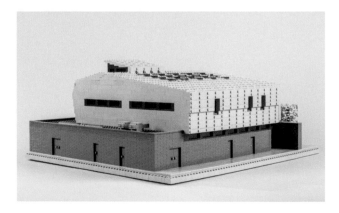

Left: Detailed back side, complete with air conditioners and exhaust vents.

Opposite, clockwise from top left: "Big Blue," the nickname of Rescue Company 3.

Note the garage door to the right has windows in it while the door to the left does not.

A great shot of street level showcasing the detailing around the garage doors as well as the custom printed murals on the doors.

Full front shot of the new building.
Note to the left of the garage doors
that I interlocked the bricks on the
street level to give a brick-like effect
while on the upper level I did not
interlock them; rather, I stacked them
to give a smoother effect.

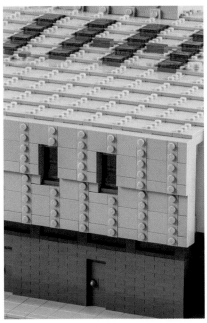

Clockwise from top: Side shot showing the different levels and the sculpting of the upper level.

Rooftop access to the HVAC units.

Side view. Note the different textures between the walls on the lower level and the walls on the upper level.

4

New York City–Inspired

LEGO Art

Much of my work is based on actual structures. Although I embellish on them and add my own stamp and signature, I'll often want to venture further outside the lines and create pieces that are interpretive, not close representations of existing structures. I am also often inspired by the works of other artists and the community that we share on Instagram. The constructions in this section represent this artistic approach. In fact, as I explain in great detail, two of them were inspired by acclaimed artists.

A Vanishing Brooklyn

Completed: **May 2016**	Approximate Number of LEGO Pieces: **4,200**	Dimensions: **15"L × 21"W × 20"H** **(38cm × 53cm × 51cm)**

A Vanishing Brooklyn was the first in an unexpected series of works that speak to change in urban neighborhoods and urban renewal. While I believe this piece is a bit overdramatic when it comes to Brooklyn, through my travels for exhibits in other American cities I find it is quite relevant.

Older buildings are being replaced with newer ones, and we're losing a lot of architectural history and aesthetic vision as a result. In some cities, though, I've been pleased to find that older facades have been maintained and new architecture built either within or on top of an existing building, creating an eye-catching mix of the two styles while meeting new standards and updating amenities.

My piece was inspired by a work that my friend artist Dylan Goldberger created: a brownstone building on which a squeegee whitewashes newer architecture. I immediately knew I wanted to render this concept in LEGO bricks, but I didn't feel that a LEGO created squeegee would necessarily resonate with an audience or present itself in a manner that could be interpreted correctly without explanation. I needed an alternative.

I had been creating some organic and flowing forms at the time and quickly determined that I'd like to approach this piece utilizing some of these natural shapes. This in turn resulted in the concept of the newer architecture crashing down on the older brownstone building, with plumes of debris exploding outward from the force. Using a technique of exposed studs on the waves of debris added perfectly to the crumbling and exploding effect. They are a textural contrast with the smooth walls and other smooth areas of the piece. Details such as the trees on the roof and the flowers in the window boxes add just a hint of contrast, color, and life to the overall piece.

Above: A brownstone stoop. Many people hang out on their stoops in the evenings.

Opposite, clockwise from top: Trees, box gardens, and bushes provide hints of life to an otherwise minimalist-style rooftop of the newer architecture.

This shot of the back side captures the crushing wave of debris quite well.

Note the use of the two different versions of the color dark gray in the lower side section.

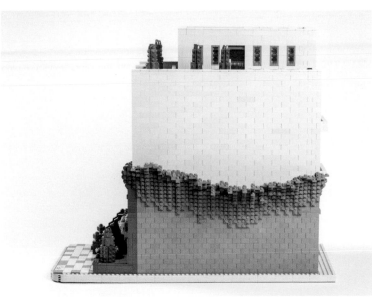

Window flower box and tree

A simple tree and window flower box are among the small details that can help bring a piece to life.

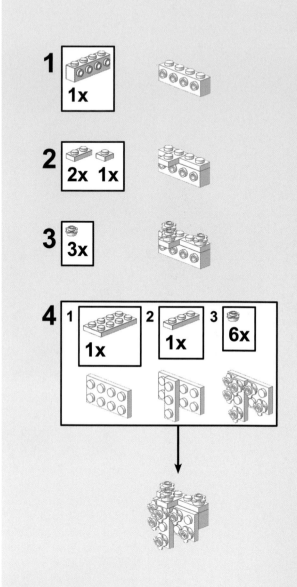

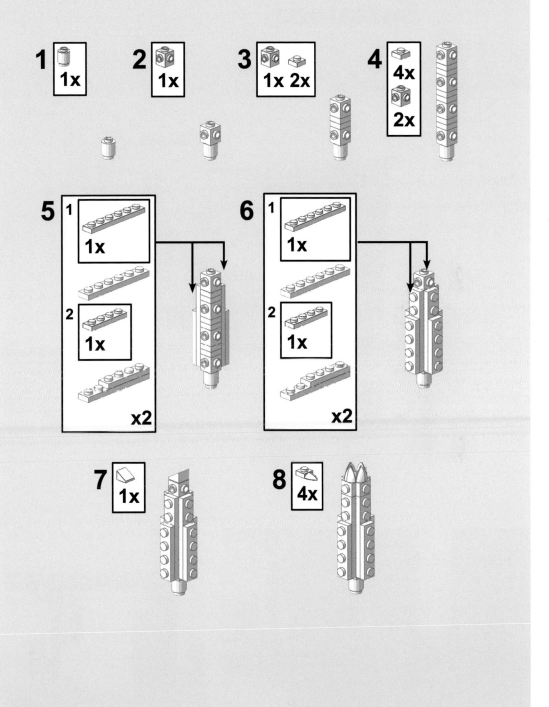

Brooklyn
Sustained

Completed:
August 2016

Approximate
Number of
LEGO Pieces:
3,900

Dimensions:
12"L × 29"W × 18"H
(31cm × 74cm × 46cm)

Shortly after I created *A Vanishing Brooklyn*, an artist I respect and follow on Instagram named Vincent Lelièvre shared a sketch of a building, and it became the basis for my work *Brooklyn Sustained*. I wanted to continue and expand upon the theme of *A Vanishing Brooklyn*. This piece depicts a facade of older architecture complemented in the body of the building by modern architecture. Achieving the detailing on the facade was a bit tricky in some areas, specifically on the top-floor level. I'd had the design technique that I used for the top floor in mind for a few years but hadn't yet fully developed it to make it workable. Working on *Brooklyn Sustained* gave me the opportunity to sort it out and I am really pleased with the outcome. Additional details, such as the outdoor spiral staircase and the green roof, accent this piece nicely without creating too much distraction.

Opposite, bottom left: A window flower box. I enjoy including flowers and other plants in my work because I feel they give my creations natural vitality and bring them to life. The brighter colors also add a nice contrast to the earth-tone colors used in the structures.

Opposite, bottom right: I always wanted a wrought-iron spiral staircase in my apartment. I built one on this piece instead.

Below: Grassy areas and gardens on the roof add to the urban-renewal aspect of this piece.

Facade detail

This facade detail represents some of my favorite work. It was tough to figure out just how to design this to achieve the texture I envisioned, but I was able to do it exactly as I had hoped.

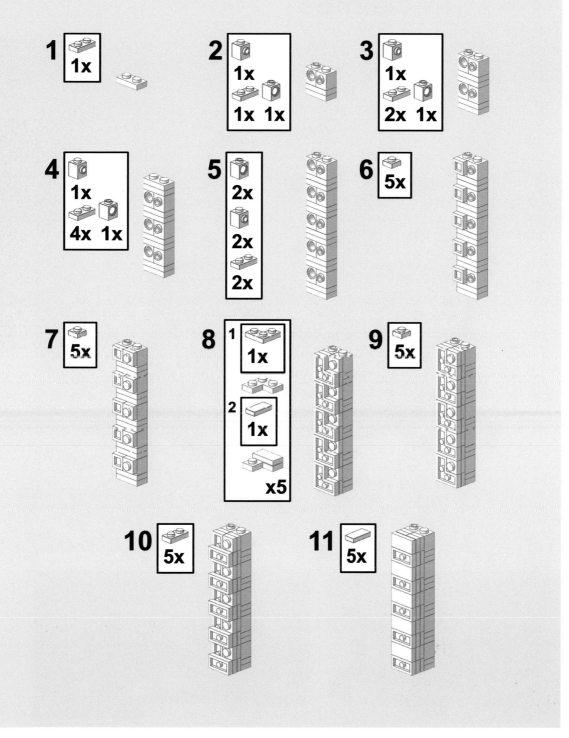

Brooklyn
Reclaimed

Completed:
March 2018

Approximate
Number of
LEGO Pieces:
4,400

Dimensions:
26"L × 15"W × 20"H
(66cm × 38cm × 51cm)

Below: This shot shows the top portion that was built onto the building. You can note the distinct differing architecture by comparing the top section to the bottom section.

Opposite, below: Street-level details: flowers, doors, wrought-iron fencing, trees, and lampposts.

I tend to work in series of three. So to round out and possibly finalize the series that started with *A Vanishing Brooklyn*, I developed *Brooklyn Reclaimed*. This piece was inspired by a building on the corner of Nevins and Pacific Streets whose outer facade was fully maintained while the inner portions had been entirely rebuilt. An area on the second floor was left as an outdoor hallway behind three open windows in the facade. This feature is one of the elements that enticed me to use this building for inspiration.

This piece is roughly the same scale as *A Vanishing Brooklyn* and *Brooklyn Sustained* and prominently utilizes the texture provided by exposing the undersides of the LEGO pieces in the facade. This is currently one of my favorite design techniques. And, as in much of my work, I have complemented the dark orange earth-tone building and gray sidewalk with little pops of color and contrast in the bushes, trees, and flowers. On the back side of the building, I've included roof-decks and trellises as details.

High Line:
Then and Now

Completed: **June 2018**	Approximate Number of LEGO Pieces: **16,200**	Dimensions: **34"L x 33"W x 24"H** **(86cm x 84cm x 61cm)**

The High Line is a former elevated freight rail line in Manhattan that runs from the West Village through Chelsea and up to West 34th Street. It is now an urban park, representing a fantastic repurposing of existing infrastructure, and offers the exact sort of contrast that catches my artistic eye in an urban environment: an elevated platform of manmade steel and brick-and-mortar buildings brought together with plants and trees. This presents an ideal visual urban setting. It was thrilling to watch this project develop over the years.

I moved to New York in 1990, and back then the High Line and the blocks that surround it were quite different than they are today. It was not so long ago that the area was one to be traversed with caution. In rendering my piece *High Line: Then and Now*, I wanted to touch on the area's transformation and capture the contrast between the two time periods. I utilized the intersection of 10th Avenue and West 23rd Street as my concept point, with the left-hand side of my piece representing "Then" and the right-hand side representing "Now." "Then" includes a run-down gas station, a decrepit parking lot, and a hollowed-out former warehouse in addition to a decaying streetscape with a stripped car up on blocks. "Now," by contrast, features clean streets, a dedicated bike lane, trees, a gallery, and a bistro. Both sections have the High Line running through them: In "Then" it is a rusting and decaying hulk of steel, and in "Now" a polished and refined presentation that reflects its current state.

Note the transition from an overgrown
and junk-filled High Line to the neater,
manicured pathway of the current park.

Clockwise, from top: Facing eastward on 23rd Street.

The iconic New York City water tower.

The walking path, facing south.

Pool
Hall

Completed:
November 2011

Approximate
Number of
LEGO Pieces:
550

Dimensions:
6"L × 15"W × 8"H
(15cm × 38cm × 20cm)

Pool Hall is another one of my older pieces in this book. It is not based
on an actual building but instead represents the soul of a gritty and run-down
neighborhood structure. My design and aesthetic goal was to create a piece
that evokes the feeling of a locale that has seen better days—and to do
so in a medium that is mostly known to be a shiny, happy, bright-colored
children's toy. The key to success was the palette I used, balancing the
brick-orange and light gray sidings, the latter evoking mortar cracking and
peeling away from the exposed brick, all against the weathered green
of the front facade. This was a pivotal piece for me in that it established that
I could indeed re-create my vision of gritty urban realism utilizing LEGO
bricks as the artistic medium.

Left: This angled
side shot shows
the overall weath-
ering effect and
different colors
and textures
of this piece.

Opposite: Frontal
shot showing
lots of dif-
ferent building
techniques. The
windows in the
bottom area are
built sideways.
The "POOL" sign
is constructed
entirely with
LEGO bricks; it
is not printed.

Glossary

 brick: The staple of the LEGO building system. Bricks come in various sizes and are measured by the number and position of their studs. The most iconic LEGO brick is the 2 × 4.

 **brick with side studs:** These bricks permit building sideways. Building sideways allows for very fine details to be obtained.

 hinge plate: The hinge plate makes it possible to create interesting angles on building walls.

 jumper plate: The jumper plate is a 1 × 2 plate, but with a stud in the center of it. This piece is integral to creating small details and indentations. I use these extensively in my work.

 **leaf piece:** This is the LEGO leaf element. I also use altBricks leaf pieces to complement the LEGO leaf piece, because they are available in a wider variety of colors.

plate: LEGO plates are one-third the height of LEGO bricks but, like bricks, are otherwise measured by the number and position of their studs.

Technic brick: I use these types of bricks to embed the studs of plates. This allows for the undersides of the plates to be exposed and creates a very satisfactory detail on the facades and cornices of my buildings.

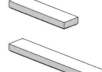

tile: LEGO tiles are the same height as plates but do not have studs on top of them. These are used for creating smooth surfaces such as sidewalks. Tiles also have a slight notch at the bottom of each side. These notches add an excellent textural detail to pieces. I used this notch detail extensively on the facade of *Bronx: Rescue 3 (Then)* (page 162).

Acknowledgments

There are a good number of people who helped in the creation of this book and also had an integral voice in some of the milestones in my art career. I cannot thank the following enough for their support, for their guidance, and for believing in me and my work over the years.

First, I'd like to thank my editor, Garrett McGrath, and publisher, Michael Sand, as well as the entire Abrams team; my agent extraordinaire, Susan Hawk at Upstart Crow Literary; and Bryan Regan for the amazing photo shoots and the laughs we shared while shooting.

I could not have accomplished any of this without the initial push, guidance, and confidence boost from my friend Kirk Benshoff.

Thank you to the BrickUniverse Convention Management Team: Greyson, Angela, Gaylon, Lauren, York, and Roland Beights for the endless opportunities and support and for believing in me as an artist.

To Joe Meno for the instruction panels and for always being a great supporter. Rocco Buttliere for the Digital Designer expertise and so much more. Bruce Johanns for the support and encouragement during the Brooklyn years. Rusty von Dyl, my artistic soulmate in San Diego. Tommy and Elaine Armstrong for the printed bricks and many laughs. Artists Dylan Goldberger and Vincent Lelièvre for the inspiration.

To Christine Ma, Erin Stein, Ian Mayer, Albert Chau, Andy Bryant, Lia Chan, Vin and Maria Tabone, Paul Hetherington, Sid Dinsay, Nick Fickou, and my friends and colleagues in the book publishing industry: Your support has been immeasurable.

Very special thanks to my family in Massachusetts.

And, of course, to Marcie for accepting my creative whims and my never-ending hustle.

Lastly, my fans: Without you, this book and the guy who created this work would not be here. Thank you for all of your support at conventions, at exhibitions, and on social media! See you soon!

Photographer: Bryan Regan
Instruction panel creation: Joe Meno
Brick Graphics: Rusty von Dyl
Printed Bricks: Tommy and Elaine Armstrong